Veni, Vidi, Vici: Conquering The Struggles Of Modern Life

JULIAN KANE

Published by JULIAN KANE, 2024.

Table of Contents

Introduction: The Battle Within

In a world that constantly demands more from us—more productivity, more connection, more success—it's easy to forget that the most significant battles we face are not on the outside. They are the quiet, invisible struggles within ourselves. The *battle within* is not one fought with weapons or words, but with our own fears, anxieties, insecurities, and doubts. It's the battle between who we are and who we feel we are supposed to be. It's the war we wage with our own minds, hearts, and souls every single day.

The Invisible War of the Modern World

To the outside world, it seems like we have it all together. Our social media profiles showcase carefully curated moments of happiness, success, and beauty. We wake up, go to work, attend to responsibilities, check off tasks, and interact with those around us. On the surface, life can seem efficient, seamless, even perfect. But beneath this veneer, many of us are fighting a war no one can see—a war that takes place not on a battlefield but in the mind, the body, and the spirit.

This invisible battle has become more pronounced in the modern world. We live in an era of hyper-connectivity, where information is constantly bombarding us from all directions, where expectations—societal, familial, personal—are set higher than ever before. We are expected to be constantly available, always achieving, never resting. The pressure is relentless, and it's wearing us down.

Yet, it's not just the external pressures that make this battle so formidable. It's how we internalize these demands, how we allow the weight of the world to take root within us. We question ourselves. We doubt our worth. We feel like impostors in our own lives. We fear failure, and we fear judgment—often more than we fear anything else.

The Desire for Triumph: Veni, Vidi, Vici

It is in this very context that the ancient phrase "Veni, Vidi, Vici"—"I came, I saw, I conquered"—resonates so deeply with us. These words were uttered by Julius Caesar after a swift and decisive victory. For Caesar, this was a moment of triumphant conquest, a declaration of his dominance over the challenges he faced.

But today, in the context of our personal lives, these words represent something more: a framework for how we can overcome the struggles we face within ourselves. What if we could take Caesar's words and apply them not just to military victories, but to the day-to-day battles we fight in our own minds? What if "coming" meant recognizing our challenges, "seeing" meant understanding them, and "conquering" meant developing the resilience and the tools to overcome them?

This book is a journey towards that kind of victory. It is not about the conquest of external forces, but the conquest of our internal battles—the struggles of identity, purpose, fear, and resilience that we face in today's world. Just as Caesar moved swiftly and decisively to conquer his enemies, we too can learn to approach our own battles with clarity, purpose, and strength.

The Rise of Internal Struggles

The challenges we face today are not just personal inconveniences; they are deeply rooted in the fabric of modern life. We are living in an age where technology has altered the very nature of how we experience time and space. In the past, battles were fought on physical terrain. Today, they are fought within the realms of our minds and emotions.

We live in a world that is simultaneously more connected and more isolating than ever. The digital revolution has made communication faster and more global, yet it has also introduced a new kind of isolation—the feeling of being constantly alone in a crowd. Social media platforms, while offering instant access to others, often create a sense of alienation as we compare our lives to the curated, filtered versions we see online. The pressure to present a perfect image can leave us feeling disconnected from our true selves.

Mental health struggles, including anxiety and depression, are at all-time highs. People report feeling overwhelmed by the demands of everyday life, unsure how to cope with the pressures that come from all angles. The quest for success, self-improvement, and social validation can leave us feeling perpetually exhausted, always chasing the next achievement without ever feeling truly fulfilled.

And yet, it's not just external factors that contribute to this sense of inner turmoil. Many of us battle a deep-seated fear of failure, an irrational belief that we are not enough, or that we are destined to fall short of our potential. We often internalize the expectations placed upon us by others, measuring our worth through the lens of comparison and competition.

The Concept of "Veni, Vidi, Vici" in Modern Context

In the context of the battles we face today, "Veni, Vidi, Vici" becomes more than a triumphant declaration. It becomes a call to arms—a rallying cry for those who wish to overcome the internal struggles that define modern life. It represents a mindset shift, from feeling like a victim of circumstances to taking proactive control of one's life.

1. **Veni – Coming to Terms with the Struggle**

The first step in any battle is showing up. In this case, it's about coming to terms with the challenges we face within ourselves. It's about recognizing the weight of the pressures that have been building over time. Coming is about being honest with ourselves. We must acknowledge our vulnerabilities, our fears, and the factors that have contributed to our sense of defeat. We cannot conquer what we are unwilling to face.

This is a crucial step because, for many, the hardest part of the struggle is simply acknowledging that we're in a battle at all. Many of us push our emotions and doubts aside, hoping they will disappear or solve themselves. But the truth is, they only grow stronger when ignored. Recognizing the battle is the first victory.

1. **Vidi – Understanding the Depth of the Battle**

Once we have come to terms with our struggles, the next step is to see them clearly. Understanding the true nature of our challenges allows us to develop the right strategies for conquering them. This is where awareness becomes key. In this phase, we examine the root causes of our struggles—be it societal pressures, self-doubt, or fear of failure. We ask ourselves the hard questions: What is really holding us back? Why do we feel trapped?

The act of seeing is not simply about identifying the problem but about understanding its full complexity. We begin to unravel the narrative that has been written for us and instead, we write our own story.

1. Vici – Conquering with Clarity and Resilience

Conquering is about taking decisive action. It's not enough to recognize and understand the challenges—we must actively engage with them, break them down, and rise above them. This requires clarity of mind and resilience of spirit. We need tools, strategies, and mental fortitude to overcome the internal forces that keep us from moving forward.

But conquering doesn't just mean defeating the struggle—it's about transforming the struggle into a stepping stone for growth. Every battle we face is an opportunity to learn, to adapt, and to emerge stronger than before. The true victory is not just in overcoming the obstacle, but in how we are changed by the process.

The Journey Ahead

In this book, we will explore these themes in depth, unraveling the internal struggles that define modern life and offering strategies for overcoming them. We will take a journey through the complex landscape of personal identity, mental resilience, and emotional well-being. Each chapter will equip you with the tools to come to terms with your challenges, understand their root causes, and ultimately, conquer them—so that you can live with greater clarity, purpose, and peace.

This is not just a book about surviving the modern world—it's a guide to thriving within it. And like Caesar's declaration, it's a call to arms for all of us to rise above the inner battles we face and emerge victorious.

Chapter 1: The Coming –
Recognizing the Battle

The Rise of Invisible Battles

In the early hours of the morning, as the world slowly comes to life, many of us find ourselves already caught in the grip of a battle. But unlike the wars of history, these struggles don't unfold on a battlefield with visible markers of victory or defeat. They are quiet, subtle, and often invisible to the outside world. And yet, their impact is profound, shaping not only our days but our very sense of self.

This is the nature of modern life: the internal battles that simmer beneath the surface. These are the challenges that don't come with loud declarations of war. Instead, they creep into our consciousness when we least expect them, often disguised as fleeting thoughts or unnoticed anxieties. They are the struggles we carry in our hearts and minds—the silent wars fought in the spaces between waking and sleeping, in moments of self-doubt, in the fear of not being enough.

Our daily battles are fought on multiple fronts. There's the pressure of achieving more—more at work, more in our relationships, more in our personal development. There's the constant comparison, the need to measure up to others, even when we don't know the full story behind their seemingly perfect lives. We're surrounded by an ever-present sense of urgency, as though we must constantly prove our worth to ourselves and to the world. And all of this is compounded by the rapid pace of change in our world—technology that advances faster than we can adapt, societal expectations that evolve constantly, and a culture that promotes success as the ultimate goal, often without offering a clear path to it.

It is easy to forget that these invisible struggles are a natural part of the human experience. In a world that celebrates achievement and visibility, it's easy to overlook the quiet battles that happen in the background of our lives. We don't often talk about the mental fatigue that comes from juggling responsibilities, or the emotional weight of trying to live up to impossible standards. We don't always acknowledge the toll that chronic stress takes on our bodies and minds. These are the battles we fight alone, in silence, because they are not always recognized by the world around us.

But just because these struggles are invisible doesn't make them any less real. The anxiety that rises in the chest when you open your email inbox, the exhaustion that settles in after a day of social interactions, the constant pressure of needing to perform—these are not just fleeting inconveniences. They are battles. And they are fought by millions every day.

What makes these struggles particularly insidious is their ability to go unnoticed, both by others and by ourselves. We become so accustomed to living with the weight of these internal wars that we forget they are even happening. We learn to push through the discomfort, to ignore the mental chatter, and to keep moving forward, believing that if we just keep going, the battles will resolve themselves. But in truth, this only deepens the fight. By neglecting to recognize these struggles, we make it harder to address them, and they quietly erode our sense of well-being.

In many ways, the invisible nature of these battles makes them more challenging to navigate. Unlike physical battles, where the stakes are clear and the consequences tangible, the internal struggles are often less definable. We might not be able to pinpoint exactly what's wrong, but we know something isn't right. There's a vague sense of unease, a constant feeling that we're fighting against something—though it's hard to say what. It's the pressure to perform, to be perfect, to be everything to everyone. It's the fear of failure that lurks just below the surface, the nagging feeling that we're never quite doing enough, never quite enough ourselves.

These battles aren't confined to a particular age or stage in life. They affect us all, in different ways, at different times. Young professionals entering the workforce face the pressure of proving themselves in a competitive landscape. Parents balancing careers and family life wrestle with guilt and the fear of not being present enough for their children. Retirees, too, face their own set of invisible struggles—grappling with the loss of purpose, the shifting of identity, and the fear of being forgotten. And in between these phases, there are moments of self-doubt, uncertainty, and quiet crises of faith that we all encounter.

In the past, these struggles might have been easier to dismiss. There was less pressure to talk about them openly, and fewer resources to help navigate them. But today, we find ourselves in a world that is both more connected and more isolated than ever before. We have more access to information, more ways to communicate, and more ways to share our lives with others. But we also have more distractions, more comparisons, and more expectations. The world moves at a pace that leaves little time for reflection, and we find ourselves constantly on the go, responding to others, reacting to circumstances, and rarely taking a moment to just *be*.

The modern struggle is not just about external forces; it is the way these forces infiltrate our minds and emotions, shaping how we feel about ourselves and our place in the world. We no longer just fight for survival; we fight for significance. We are caught in a battle to be heard, to be valued, to be seen. And because these struggles often go unnoticed by others, we end up feeling like we are in this fight alone.

But it doesn't have to be this way. Recognizing these internal battles is the first step in reclaiming our power. The act of naming our struggles—of acknowledging that they are real and valid—is a victory in itself. It allows us to step out of the shadows and into a place where we can begin to make sense of what's happening. And once we understand the nature of the battle, we can start to develop strategies for fighting it.

In many ways, the first battle we need to win is against our own denial. We must stop pretending that these struggles don't exist or that they will simply go away on their own. It's time to stop ignoring the mental and emotional fatigue we feel each day. It's time to stop pretending that we have to carry the weight of the world alone.

Once we acknowledge the battle, we can begin to equip ourselves with the tools and strategies needed to face it. The journey ahead is one of understanding, of learning how to manage the internal forces that have kept us in conflict. This is the work of conquering the invisible battles—by not just surviving them, but by thriving in the midst of them.

The internal battle may never completely fade away, but with awareness, resilience, and the right mindset, we can turn it into a force for growth, strength, and transformation. It's time to recognize these struggles for what they truly are: not obstacles to our happiness, but opportunities for our personal evolution. And in doing so, we can find our way to victory—not just in the battles we face, but in the lives we are destined to create.

The Global Exhaustion Epidemic

We live in an era where exhaustion has become a silent epidemic—one that doesn't just impact a few but reaches across the globe, affecting people from all walks of life. It's the kind of exhaustion that can't be measured by how many hours we sleep, nor is it solved by a weekend getaway or a vacation. This is a deep, pervasive weariness, the kind that seeps into our bones and our minds, leaving us feeling both physically drained and mentally empty.

It's a strange paradox of our times: we're more connected than ever before, with instant access to information, communication, and opportunity. And yet, the more connected we become, the more we seem to lose our sense of connection to ourselves. The pace of life has quickened to a point where it feels as though we're always "on," perpetually running to keep up, never quite able to catch our breath.

Exhaustion in this modern age isn't just about the physical act of being tired. It's a collective fatigue, one that's mental, emotional, and even spiritual. It's the weariness of constant pressure, of the need to perform and achieve, and the stress of balancing competing priorities without ever feeling like we're doing enough. It's the weight of expectations—self-imposed and external—that pulls us down, the unrelenting sense that we're falling short in a world that constantly demands more.

In many ways, we've become addicted to exhaustion. The hustle culture, which encourages us to "rise and grind" and "never stop," has become not just a philosophy, but a way of life. The glorification of busyness has made it feel almost wrong to take a moment for rest or reflection. We push ourselves harder, believing that if we keep going, we'll eventually catch up or make up for what we missed. But the truth is, the harder we push, the more exhausted we become, until we reach a point where even the idea of rest feels foreign, even unattainable.

This epidemic of exhaustion is not confined to one particular group or region. It stretches across borders, age groups, and industries. Young professionals, overwhelmed by the expectations of the modern workplace, feel the weight of burnout pressing on them at an early age. Parents juggling careers and family obligations can't remember the last time they had time to themselves, constantly putting the needs of others ahead of their own. Students, facing the pressure to succeed academically, are bogged down by the weight of performance anxiety and the fear of not measuring up. Even those in retirement or later life struggle with feelings of purposelessness and an inability to relax, caught in the struggle to maintain relevance in a rapidly changing world.

The pervasiveness of exhaustion is made all the more challenging by the fact that it's often invisible. On the outside, we appear fine. We go through the motions of daily life, checking off our to-do lists, participating in social engagements, and fulfilling our responsibilities. But inside, the toll is undeniable. We feel worn thin, spread too thin, with little left to give. This kind of exhaustion doesn't always show up as visible signs of fatigue; rather, it manifests as a kind of quiet depletion, a numbness that settles into our daily routines, making everything feel like a chore.

It's also important to recognize that this exhaustion is not only a consequence of working too much, but also of living in an overstimulated environment. The constant influx of information, the never-ending notifications, and the pressure to stay updated can quickly overwhelm our senses. We are expected to be present in every conversation, on top of every news story, and constantly engaged with an ever-expanding web of digital connections. But in doing so, we lose sight of our own internal landscape. We disconnect from what truly matters to us, drowning in the noise of the world around us.

Our bodies, too, are not immune to the effects of this modern exhaustion. The physical toll of constant stress manifests in subtle ways—tight shoulders, headaches, disturbed sleep patterns, and an overall sense of fatigue that doesn't seem to fade, no matter how much rest we get. Our nervous systems are in a perpetual state of fight or flight, primed for action, but rarely given the opportunity to recover and reset. We've traded true rest for temporary distractions, never allowing ourselves the space to heal and replenish.

The exhaustion epidemic also feeds on our sense of inadequacy. It's no longer enough to simply "do" things; we must do them faster, better, and more efficiently. Our productivity is constantly measured, and our worth is often tied to how much we accomplish in a day. There's always something more to be done, another goal to be achieved, another expectation to meet. We find ourselves racing against an invisible clock, one that never stops ticking, even when we need a moment of respite.

And then there's the emotional toll of this fatigue. Constant exhaustion doesn't just make us physically tired—it drains us emotionally as well. We find ourselves more irritable, less patient, and more disconnected from the people around us. Relationships, both personal and professional, begin to feel like an additional burden, a responsibility we don't have the energy to carry. We withdraw from the things we love, from the people who matter most, because there simply isn't enough energy to give. The feeling of being drained becomes all-encompassing, and the idea of rejuvenating ourselves feels as distant as a far-off dream.

This exhaustion epidemic is not something we can simply sleep off. It's a deep-rooted issue that requires more than just rest—it requires a shift in how we approach our lives. It demands a reckoning with how we've allowed external pressures to shape our internal realities, and a recalibration of our priorities.

But there is hope. The first step in confronting this global epidemic is acknowledging it. We must stop pretending that we're invincible, that we can push through it all without consequence. We need to understand that true rest isn't just about taking a break from work or obligations, but about reconnecting with ourselves, restoring our sense of balance, and allowing our bodies and minds the space they need to recover. This requires more than just "time off"—it requires a fundamental change in how we view productivity, success, and the pursuit of happiness.

Recognizing the symptoms of exhaustion is crucial to overcoming it. We must learn to listen to our bodies and our minds, to honor the limits they place on us, and to give ourselves permission to rest when we need it. We need to create space for reflection, to pause and evaluate what truly matters in our lives, and to let go of the pressure to do it all.

The global exhaustion epidemic is a symptom of a society that values constant motion over mindful presence, achievement over well-being. But it doesn't have to be this way. We have the power to redefine what it means to live a fulfilling life—not by doing more, but by doing what truly matters with purpose, intention, and clarity. We can choose to step off the treadmill of constant striving and find peace in the quiet moments of simply *being*.

This is where true recovery begins—not in the absence of exhaustion, but in our ability to face it, understand it, and reclaim our sense of balance in a world that often demands too much.

The Identity Crisis of the Digital Age

We are more connected than ever before. With a few taps of our fingers, we can reach across the globe, engage in real-time conversations, and access an almost infinite pool of information. But despite this unprecedented access, the digital age has also introduced a paradoxical crisis: a profound sense of disconnection, a fragmentation of self. We find ourselves caught in a constant cycle of comparison, our identities constantly shifting and splintering in response to the images and personas we encounter online.

The digital age promises the world at our fingertips, and yet, in many ways, it has made us feel more lost than ever. The very tools designed to enhance our connectivity have become the breeding ground for one of the most significant challenges of our time: the crisis of identity.

At its core, this identity crisis is about who we are when the noise fades away. In a world where our lives are increasingly lived through digital screens, how do we hold on to a sense of self? How do we define who we are when there are so many conflicting images of success, happiness, and purpose surrounding us at every moment? And more importantly, how do we navigate a world that constantly demands more of us, often without allowing us the space to reflect on who we truly are?

Every day, we are bombarded with curated versions of life—perfectly staged photos, carefully crafted updates, influencers sharing their "authentic" selves, businesses pushing their products through hyper-targeted ads. The allure of these digital representations is undeniable. We look at these polished images and think, "If I had that, I would be happy. If I could live like that, I would feel whole." But this constant exposure to idealized lives creates an insidious tension, one that chips away at our self-worth. We begin to question our own lives, our own choices, and whether we are doing enough or living fully enough.

This is the first layer of the identity crisis: the external pressure to conform to an ideal. Social media, with its infinite scroll of "better" versions of reality, encourages us to measure ourselves against an ever-moving target. Whether it's the latest influencer sharing the perfect vacation photos or the colleague who seems to have it all—success, looks, and wealth—there's always someone out there who seems to be living a life that's more "successful," more "perfect," more "complete" than our own.

The more we compare ourselves to these images, the more disconnected we feel from our true selves. What we fail to realize is that these curated versions of reality are, for the most part, just that—curated. Behind the scenes, there is often struggle, imperfection, and hardship. Yet, the digital age doesn't leave room for these vulnerabilities. It rewards perfection, and in doing so, creates a system in which we feel compelled to constantly put forth a version of ourselves that we think others want to see.

The result? We lose touch with who we really are. The more we shape our identities based on external validation—the likes, the comments, the shares—the less we connect with the inner core of who we are. We start to ask ourselves: "Who am I when the screen goes dark?" In the silence of our own thoughts, the constant comparison begins to weigh heavily on our psyche. We lose sight of our uniqueness, of the things that make us who we truly are, and instead, become a fragmented collection of expectations, projections, and surface-level desires.

This fractured sense of self doesn't just happen overnight. It's a gradual process. Every day, the pressure to perform, to present ourselves in the best light, to chase the external markers of success, wears away at our sense of authenticity. We become conditioned to believe that our worth is determined by how we are seen by others, how many people follow us, how many likes we accumulate, how many people "approve" of us. This is not the foundation of a healthy self-concept, yet it has become the standard by which many measure their lives.

But this digital crisis of identity isn't just about social media. It's a larger phenomenon that touches every aspect of our modern lives. The digital world is everywhere: in our workplaces, our social lives, even our relationships.

Technology, while offering vast opportunities for growth and connection, has also created a world where our personal boundaries are constantly eroded. We feel the need to be constantly available, to respond instantly, to keep up with the endless flow of information. The constant barrage of notifications, emails, messages, and updates contributes to the sense of being pulled in countless directions, leaving little space for introspection or a clear sense of self.

Consider the professional world, for example. The pressure to constantly be "on" and available can make it feel impossible to separate work from personal life. Email inboxes and instant messaging apps now serve as constant reminders that we are never truly off-duty. We're constantly performing, constantly juggling, constantly trying to prove our worth. And in the process, we risk losing sight of what truly matters: our sense of purpose, our values, and our emotional well-being.

This is the second layer of the identity crisis: the erosion of boundaries. As technology seeps into every facet of our lives, it becomes harder to draw lines between work and home, between personal time and public life. The constant connectivity means that we are expected to be available at all times, and the constant flood of information makes it difficult to tune out, to turn off, and to focus on what's truly important to us.

The impact of this boundaryless existence is profound. It leads to burnout, a constant state of overextension, and a growing sense of dissatisfaction. The pressure to be everything to everyone—to maintain the perfect balance between career, family, social life, and personal pursuits—becomes overwhelming. The expectation that we should be constantly progressing, growing, and achieving leaves little room for simply being. We forget how to just exist in the moment, how to savor the here and now, without the need to document or quantify it.

The third and perhaps most insidious layer of this digital identity crisis is the existential uncertainty it fosters. With so many competing voices telling us who we should be, what we should do, and how we should live, it's easy to lose track of our own desires and values. In the rush to keep up with the demands of the digital world, we begin to ask the hardest question of all: What do *I* really want? And when we can't answer that question, we experience a deep sense of emptiness, a feeling that we are living for others, not for ourselves. This disconnection from our authentic desires leads to a profound sense of disillusionment—a feeling that, no matter how much we accomplish, something is always missing.

At the root of the crisis lies a fundamental misunderstanding of what identity truly is. Identity isn't something that can be built solely through external validation or by conforming to the latest trends or societal norms. True identity is built from within, grounded in our values, our beliefs, our desires, and our understanding of our place in the world. It is a living, breathing thing, constantly evolving, and not something that can be quantified by likes or followers.

To resolve this identity crisis, we must first reclaim ownership of our own narrative. We need to stop allowing external forces to dictate who we should be and start asking ourselves: *Who am I without the noise?* What values do I hold dear? What do I stand for, and what am I willing to fight for? These are the questions that will guide us back to our authentic selves, far beyond the pixels of a digital screen.

This process of self-discovery requires slowing down, disconnecting from the constant barrage of information, and creating space for introspection. It requires acknowledging that we don't need to conform to external expectations in order to be worthy. We are worthy simply by being ourselves.

The digital age has made it easier than ever to compare, to lose ourselves in the noise, and to feel fragmented in the process. But it has also made it possible to reconnect with our true selves. By choosing to prioritize our mental and emotional well-being, by setting boundaries and embracing our authentic values, we can rebuild our sense of identity from a place of strength and clarity.

In the end, it is not the digital world that defines us, but how we choose to engage with it. It is possible to navigate this age of constant connection without losing ourselves. The key is in remembering who we are at our core, and standing firm in the face of a world that constantly tries to tell us otherwise. Reclaiming our identity in the digital age is not a passive act—it is a deliberate choice, a commitment to authenticity in the face of external pressures. It is the battle to not just survive the digital age, but to thrive within it, as the best version of ourselves.

The Tyranny of Choice

We live in an age of unparalleled abundance—an era where choice is no longer a luxury but a pervasive, almost overwhelming force. From the smallest decisions about what to eat or wear, to the grander choices about career paths and life partners, we are constantly faced with a myriad of options. On the surface, this seems like a great boon. Who wouldn't want the freedom to choose, to shape their own life in a way that feels most authentic? And yet, as we dive deeper into the paradox of choice, it becomes clear that the very thing that should be empowering can, in fact, become one of our greatest sources of stress and dissatisfaction.

Choice, in all its glory, has a dark side. The more options we have, the more difficult it becomes to make decisions. What begins as a promise of freedom transforms into a suffocating burden. In a world where every moment presents a new decision, every action must be weighed against a plethora of alternatives, each with its own set of consequences. The sheer number of choices available to us—both trivial and life-altering—can lead to a paralyzing effect. We hesitate, overthink, and second-guess ourselves, often unable to make any decision at all.

The first sign of the tyranny of choice is what we might call decision fatigue. This phenomenon occurs when the constant need to choose wears us down mentally and emotionally. Each decision, no matter how small, requires cognitive energy, and over time, this can leave us feeling exhausted, distracted, and incapable of making decisions with confidence. The average person makes thousands of decisions each day—many of them without even realizing it. From the moment we wake up to the moment we go to bed, our brains are constantly weighing options, processing information, and trying to figure out the best course of action.

When we are bombarded with an endless array of choices, our brains can become overwhelmed, and our ability to make good decisions diminishes.

Research has shown that, when presented with too many options, people tend to avoid making a decision altogether. We fear regret, we fear making the wrong choice, and we often end up paralyzed by the very abundance that was meant to liberate us. Ironically, the more choices we have, the less satisfied we are with the choices we do make. We constantly wonder if there was a better option we overlooked, or if we could have chosen differently. In the end, we find ourselves trapped in a cycle of dissatisfaction, where the abundance of choice has led not to fulfillment, but to frustration.

This phenomenon is not just psychological; it also has profound effects on our happiness and well-being. The expectation that we should be able to make the "perfect" choice—the choice that leads to the best possible outcome—leads to a kind of chronic dissatisfaction. The pressure to choose wisely, to optimize every decision, can erode our sense of contentment. No matter how successful our choices may seem in the moment, we are haunted by the feeling that there was always a better path, a more perfect option. This dissatisfaction with our decisions can compound over time, leading to a constant state of longing for something better, something we may never be able to identify.

The tyranny of choice also extends to the idea of perfection. In a world where every decision we make has the potential to shape our future, we begin to believe that each choice must be perfect in order to lead to a perfect life. This idea is perpetuated by the image of the "ideal" life that we see portrayed on social media, in movies, and in the stories we tell ourselves. We see others making seemingly flawless choices—choices that lead to career success, romantic fulfillment, and financial prosperity. We think, if only we could make those same choices, we too would find the happiness we crave. But the truth is, there is no such thing as a perfect choice. Life is messy, unpredictable, and often requires us to make decisions with limited information, uncertain outcomes, and imperfect options.

In reality, perfectionism is a trap. The pursuit of the "perfect" decision is not only unrealistic, but it can also prevent us from making any decision at all. The fear of making a mistake, of choosing the wrong path, paralyzes us. We become stuck in a loop of indecision, constantly evaluating our options without ever committing to one. In the end, this desire for perfection can leave us feeling unfulfilled, as we squander opportunities in our attempt to avoid the discomfort of imperfection.

Perhaps the most insidious aspect of the tyranny of choice is how it exacerbates our sense of self-doubt and insecurity. In an era where we are constantly told that we can have it all—that we can achieve our dreams if we just make the right choices—the pressure to get everything right becomes suffocating. We measure our worth by the choices we make, believing that our happiness and success are directly linked to our ability to choose the "right" path. In this environment, it is easy to feel that our worth is contingent on the decisions we make, and that any misstep will result in failure.

This pressure to choose correctly is compounded by the fear of missing out (FOMO)—the anxiety that we are somehow missing the opportunity of a lifetime by not making the right choice. We fear that by choosing one path, we are closing the door on countless other possibilities, and that the road we choose today will define the rest of our lives. This fear can be paralyzing, preventing us from moving forward, from taking action, and from embracing the uncertainty that is an inherent part of life.

At its core, the tyranny of choice is rooted in a desire for control. We want to believe that, if we make the right decisions, we can control the outcome of our lives. But the truth is, control is an illusion. Life is unpredictable, and no amount of decision-making will ever guarantee us the perfect life. What we can control, however, is how we respond to the choices we make. Instead of being paralyzed by the fear of making the wrong decision, we can embrace the imperfection of our choices and find meaning in the process of choosing, rather than in the outcome.

In the face of this tyranny, the antidote is not to eliminate choices altogether, but to learn to embrace the art of simplicity. Rather than striving for perfection in every decision, we can focus on making decisions that are aligned with our core values and our purpose. By narrowing our focus and learning to let go of the pressure to make every choice a perfect one, we can free ourselves from the suffocating weight of decision fatigue and regain a sense of agency over our lives. We can choose to prioritize what truly matters—our health, our relationships, our passions—and let go of the endless pursuit of external validation or material success.

In a world that constantly presents us with an overwhelming array of choices, it is easy to forget that we do not need to make every decision perfectly. We do not need to optimize every moment, or find the "best" path. Sometimes, the act of choosing—any choice—is enough. By letting go of the tyranny of choice, we can reclaim our sense of peace, satisfaction, and joy. We can embrace the uncertainty and imperfection that is inherent in every decision and find contentment in the journey, rather than in the destination.

Consciousness and the Age of Overload

In today's world, it is almost impossible to escape the constant stream of information bombarding us. From the moment we wake up to the moment we fall asleep, our senses are flooded with notifications, emails, social media updates, advertisements, and endless news cycles. We live in an age of unparalleled connectivity, where information is at our fingertips, yet this very abundance of information—rather than empowering us—has contributed to a quiet yet profound crisis in our mental and emotional well-being.

The overload of information has created a dissonance within our consciousness. We are constantly processing data, yet this constant influx leaves little room for deep thought, introspection, or true understanding. Instead of using information as a tool for growth and enlightenment, we find ourselves drowning in it, unable to process it fully before the next wave hits. The result is a fragmented consciousness, where attention is constantly pulled in multiple directions and our ability to focus on any one thing becomes increasingly difficult.

We have all felt it—the creeping sense of disconnection. It's the feeling that, despite being constantly connected to the world around us, we are increasingly disconnected from our own thoughts, feelings, and desires. Our consciousness is no longer just a place for personal reflection and contemplation; it has become a battlefield of competing distractions. Every app, website, and platform demands our attention, and every notification pulls us away from the present moment. In the face of this onslaught, we are left with little space for true mindfulness or emotional processing. The result is a society that is perpetually distracted, constantly seeking the next bit of information or the next hit of dopamine, but never truly present in our own lives.

This age of overload has also blurred the lines between reality and virtual reality. We spend so much of our time in digital spaces—social media, online communities, virtual meetings—that it becomes increasingly difficult to discern where the digital world ends and the physical world begins. Our minds are constantly toggling between these realities, and in doing so, we lose sight of the immediate, the tangible, the real. Our minds become fragmented, split between the demands of the digital world and the needs of our physical bodies. We are pulled in two different directions, and in the process, we lose a sense of coherence and wholeness in our consciousness.

The constant bombardment of information also impacts our ability to process emotions. In the past, when faced with stress or anxiety, individuals had a chance to sit with their feelings, to reflect on them and make sense of them. Today, however, we have little time for such reflection. The moment we feel uneasy or uncertain, we turn to our phones, to our social media feeds, to the endless stream of entertainment and distraction that surrounds us. Rather than processing our emotions and allowing them to pass through us, we push them away, distracting ourselves with the noise of the world. In doing so, we deny ourselves the opportunity to heal, to grow, and to understand the true nature of our emotional responses.

One of the most insidious aspects of this overload is how it undermines our capacity for deep thinking. Human consciousness is designed to engage with information on multiple levels—intellectually, emotionally, and spiritually. But when we are bombarded by a constant flood of data, we are unable to engage with it in a meaningful way. The superficiality of this constant influx prevents us from reflecting deeply on ideas, from synthesizing information in ways that can lead to new insights. Instead, we skim, we glance, we scroll, but rarely do we engage. The consequence is a collective shallowness in our thought processes. We consume more information than ever before, yet our understanding of it becomes increasingly shallow.

This constant engagement with information also diminishes our attention span. Once, we could immerse ourselves in a book for hours, lose ourselves in a film, or have a conversation without the nagging feeling of our phones buzzing in our pockets. But today, even the simplest tasks are interrupted by constant distractions. Studies have shown that the average person's attention span has dramatically decreased in the last few decades. The more we divide our attention, the less we are able to focus on any one thing for an extended period of time. The result is a fragmented sense of self and an inability to deeply engage with the world around us. We are always looking for the next thing, the next update, the next notification, rather than remaining present in the moment.

At the same time, the overload of information exacerbates our feelings of inadequacy and self-doubt. The digital world, with its curated representations of success and happiness, presents an image of life that is often far removed from reality. We scroll through our feeds, comparing our lives to the seemingly perfect lives of others. This constant comparison fuels our insecurity, making us feel as though we are falling short of some arbitrary standard of success. In truth, the information we consume does not reflect the full complexity of the human experience. Social media profiles are curated, news cycles are sensationalized, and advertisements are designed to make us feel inadequate in order to sell us something. Yet, despite knowing this, we find ourselves trapped in the cycle of comparison, constantly measuring our worth against the lives of others.

The solution to this crisis of consciousness lies in reclaiming our ability to focus and to engage with the world in a more intentional, mindful way. We must learn to set boundaries with the information we consume, to curate our digital environments in ways that support our well-being rather than undermine it. This means intentionally choosing the sources of information that we engage with, creating space in our lives for deep thinking and reflection, and allowing ourselves time to be present in the moment. In doing so, we can begin to reestablish a sense of coherence in our consciousness, allowing our thoughts, feelings, and actions to align with our true selves.

It also means allowing ourselves the grace to sit with discomfort. The digital age has conditioned us to expect instant gratification, to seek out distractions whenever we feel uncomfortable. But it is precisely in those moments of discomfort that true growth occurs. Instead of reaching for our phones or drowning out our feelings with noise, we must learn to sit with our emotions, to process them, and to let them pass. By doing so, we reclaim our emotional well-being and our ability to understand the full depth of our human experience.

In the end, the key to navigating the age of overload lies in developing a more conscious relationship with the digital world. This does not mean abandoning technology, but rather using it as a tool for intentional living. By reducing the noise and creating space for silence, reflection, and connection, we can begin to heal the fragmentation of our consciousness and reclaim our lives from the tyranny of overload. In doing so, we can not only survive this age of information, but thrive in it, finding clarity and peace amidst the noise.

Chapter 2: The Seeing – Understanding the Problem

The Concept of Time in the Modern Era

Time, once a steady, predictable force in our lives, now feels like a luxury—something we never seem to have enough of. It has become one of the most precious commodities of the modern age, and yet, ironically, we have more access to it than ever before. Technology, with all its advancements, has given us the ability to do things faster, to reach across the globe in seconds, to automate tedious tasks and streamline our efforts. Yet, despite all these conveniences, we find ourselves constantly in a race against time, feeling as if we are perpetually behind. The illusion that we have more time is just that: an illusion. What we really face is a dramatic shift in how we perceive and manage it.

The Compression of Time

In the past, time felt expansive. A day was a day. There were hours to fill with work, family, rest, and leisure. The pace of life was slower, more deliberate. We woke with the sunrise, followed a rhythm of work and rest, and often had time in between to reflect, think, and simply be. Yet, as society progressed, our perception of time began to change. The acceleration of technological advancements, the rise of instant communication, and the dominance of the digital world have all compressed time into a narrow, frantic moment. Today, a day feels like it flies by in the blink of an eye.

Consider the daily routine of a modern individual. The moment they wake, they are bombarded with notifications, emails, messages, and tasks. From the first interaction with their phone to the last glance before they sleep, time is filled with an endless series of small demands. The moment we check our phone, we're given an entire world to manage, all in the palm of our hands. These constant distractions make time feel like it's being stolen from us in bits and pieces, leaving us with a fragmented sense of the day, a sense that hours slip away without us ever fully living in them.

Yet, paradoxically, we are also told that time is on our side. There are countless articles, books, and gurus that promise we can have more time if only we manage it better—if only we optimize our schedules, automate our routines, and plan our every move. This promise, while tempting, leads to another layer of confusion about time. We are told that with all these tools at our disposal, time should be limitless, but the truth is that we're caught in an infinite loop of seeking more efficiency, while the actual experience of time continues to slip away. We are trapped in the perpetual quest for more, without ever realizing that what we truly need is not more time, but a new relationship with time itself.

Time vs. Tasks: The Illusion of Multitasking

One of the most significant illusions in the modern era is the idea of multitasking—performing multiple tasks at once in an effort to maximize productivity. In theory, multitasking is a brilliant solution to a world overflowing with things to do. Why not answer emails while making breakfast, respond to texts during meetings, or listen to a podcast while walking? The assumption is that by splitting our attention, we can accomplish more in less time. In reality, however, multitasking is a myth. Our brains are not built for true multitasking; instead, they are designed for single-task focus. When we try to juggle several things at once, we only increase cognitive load, leading to mistakes, distractions, and a sense of time moving even faster, without truly completing anything.

Studies have shown that the more we multitask, the more fragmented our experience of time becomes. We lose the ability to deeply engage with any one task, and our sense of accomplishment diminishes. The truth is, multitasking steals from us—time, attention, and fulfillment. When we devote our full attention to a single task, however, we not only do it more effectively, but we also experience a deeper connection with that activity. Time, in this sense, becomes richer, more meaningful, and more aligned with our goals. It's not about cramming more into the same amount of time; it's about consciously choosing where to spend our energy.

The Speed of Technology and the Erosion of Patience

Another major factor in the shift of our relationship with time is the acceleration of technology. The rise of digital communication has made it possible to send messages instantaneously, access information with a few taps, and complete complex tasks at the speed of thought. Yet, this increased speed comes at a cost: it erodes patience. We expect immediate results, and when they don't come, we feel frustrated and overwhelmed.

The constant push for speed creates a false sense of urgency. Everything must be done now—there is no room for waiting, reflecting, or sitting in the discomfort of time's passage. This rush to accomplish tasks as quickly as possible breeds anxiety and dissatisfaction. We begin to feel like there's never enough time because we're always chasing the next moment, always rushing toward the next task.

Ironically, the faster things get, the more we seem to miss out on the richness of the present. We are so focused on the finish line that we forget to enjoy the journey. As time accelerates, we lose the ability to savor the moments, to sit with our thoughts, or to experience the present without distraction. The rush to get things done leads to a disconnection from the deeper experience of life.

Reclaiming Time: The Power of Presence

So, how can we reclaim time? The first step is to stop thinking of time as something to be conquered or optimized. We must shift from seeing time as an adversary—something that slips through our fingers and causes us to fall behind—and begin viewing it as a tool, a precious resource that, when managed mindfully, can serve our deeper purposes.

To reclaim time, we must return to the present moment. This isn't about adding more hours to the day or squeezing in more tasks—it's about fully inhabiting the moments we have. It's about learning to engage with the present, rather than being trapped in the cycle of always thinking about what's next. The practice of mindfulness—bringing full attention to the task at hand, whether it's writing an email or enjoying a conversation—restores depth and meaning to the experience of time.

One of the most powerful ways to reclaim time is to engage in deep work—the practice of working on a single task for an uninterrupted period of time. This means setting aside time for the things that truly matter, and not allowing the distractions of the digital world to intrude. When we focus fully on a task, we not only do it better but we also experience time in a way that is far more fulfilling. Deep work allows us to fully enter a state of flow, where time feels expansive, effortless, and productive.

The power of presence also extends to our relationships. In an age where we are constantly distracted, we often give our loved ones only fragments of our attention. To truly connect with others, we must be present—physically and mentally. This means putting away our phones, shutting off distractions, and dedicating time to fully engage with the people who matter most. It's in these moments of undistracted presence that we experience time's deepest richness.

Reevaluating Priorities: Quality Over Quantity

Another key aspect of reclaiming time is to reevaluate how we spend it. Modern life often pressures us to fill every moment with activity—to be productive, efficient, and successful at all times. But in reality, we are far better off when we focus on quality over quantity. It's not about cramming more tasks into the day, but about investing our time in activities that are truly meaningful.

This shift from quantity to quality means making conscious choices about how we allocate our time. It's about asking ourselves: Does this activity bring me joy, growth, or fulfillment? If not, is it worth my time? This doesn't mean that every moment of the day must be filled with joy or excitement, but it does mean that we must be intentional about how we spend our time, ensuring that we are not wasting it on things that don't align with our values.

The Power of Saying No

In reclaiming time, one of the most powerful skills we can develop is the ability to say no. Modern life is filled with demands and expectations from every corner. We are expected to be available at all times, to take on more responsibilities, to fulfill others' needs. Yet, if we are to protect our time and our well-being, we must learn to say no—to set boundaries that honor our time and our energy. Saying no is not about being selfish; it's about preserving the space we need for what truly matters. It's about creating room in our lives for deep work, meaningful connections, and self-care.

Time as a Resource for Conquest

Reclaiming time is crucial in the battle to conquer life's challenges. Time, when used intentionally, becomes our greatest ally. It is not a finite resource to be squeezed into every corner of life; it is a canvas upon which we can create the masterpiece of our lives. By focusing on presence, quality, and intentionality, we reclaim time as a tool for growth, transformation, and true success.

In the end, the key to conquering time's challenges lies not in trying to control it, but in learning how to flow with it. By redefining our relationship with time, we begin to experience life in a way that is deeper, more fulfilling, and more aligned with our true purpose. Time, when reclaimed, becomes the ally in the pursuit of our greatest victories.

The Neuroplasticity of Our Minds

The human brain is an extraordinary organ, constantly adapting, learning, and reconfiguring itself. This ability, known as neuroplasticity, is one of the brain's most powerful features, enabling us to respond to challenges, cope with stress, and even reshape our habits. In the face of modern life's increasingly complex demands, understanding and harnessing neuroplasticity is more than a scientific curiosity—it is a critical tool for navigating the pressures, frustrations, and adversity that shape our existence.

At its core, neuroplasticity refers to the brain's ability to reorganize itself by forming new neural connections throughout life. These connections are the pathways through which we think, feel, and behave. Historically, it was believed that the brain's development was largely fixed after childhood—that by adulthood, our brain function was set in stone. However, contemporary research has shattered this myth. We now know that the brain remains malleable, capable of rewiring itself well into old age. This ability allows us to recover from injury, adapt to new experiences, and, crucially, change our responses to stress and adversity.

For many, the modern world presents constant challenges: balancing work and personal life, navigating digital distractions, facing the ever-present pressure to perform, and dealing with global uncertainties. These stressors can feel overwhelming, and they often lead to ingrained habits—stress responses that feel automatic and difficult to break. However, the very process that makes these habits so deeply entrenched is the same process we can leverage to change them. Neuroplasticity gives us the power not just to survive these challenges but to thrive in them by reprogramming the way our brains respond to stress.

Adapting to Stress: The Brain's Survival Mechanism

Our brains evolved to handle stress in a very particular way. The stress response, which includes the activation of the amygdala, is part of a primal survival mechanism. When faced with a perceived threat—whether physical, emotional, or psychological—the body goes into a heightened state of alert, preparing for fight or flight. This response was vital for the survival of our ancestors, enabling them to respond quickly to danger in their environment.

However, the stressors of the modern world are vastly different from those our ancestors encountered. Today, stress is often chronic and diffuse: it comes from work pressures, social expectations, financial strain, and the constant barrage of information. While the brain's response to these modern stressors is similar to the fight-or-flight reaction, the frequency and intensity of the stress can be much higher, leading to a state of constant low-level anxiety.

Over time, repeated exposure to stress can lead to lasting changes in the brain. Chronic activation of the stress response can alter the structure and function of key brain regions involved in emotional regulation, memory, and decision-making, particularly the prefrontal cortex and hippocampus. This can result in diminished cognitive function, emotional reactivity, and difficulties in managing stress.

Yet, in this very process of adaptation, lies the key to transformation. The brain's ability to reorganize itself means that, even under chronic stress, it is possible to reshape the neural circuits that have become wired for anxiety, worry, and overreaction. By understanding neuroplasticity, we can not only recover from the damaging effects of stress but also rewire our brains to handle adversity more effectively.

Neuroplasticity: A Tool for Habit Change

One of the most profound applications of neuroplasticity is in the realm of habit formation. Our brains love habits—patterns of behavior that we repeat automatically. These patterns are ingrained in our neural pathways, which are reinforced each time we engage in a particular behavior. Habits, whether positive or negative, are the result of repeated stimuli and responses that create lasting connections in the brain.

For example, if we consistently respond to stress by reaching for unhealthy coping mechanisms, such as eating junk food or procrastinating, the brain strengthens the neural pathways associated with these behaviors. Over time, these habits can become automatic, even though they may not serve us well.

The process is subtle and insidious, as the brain continually reinforces the behaviors that we repeat, making them more difficult to break.

But neuroplasticity offers a way out. The key is to understand that the brain is not set in stone. Just as habits are formed through repetition, they can also be undone. The process of rewiring the brain involves consciously replacing old habits with new ones, making healthier responses to stress and adversity just as automatic. This takes time and consistent effort, but the brain's malleability means that change is possible.

For example, let's say someone has developed the habit of reaching for a sugary snack whenever they feel stressed. This habit has become hardwired in their brain's reward system, and it feels automatic whenever stress arises. However, by consciously replacing this habit with a healthier alternative—such as taking a few deep breaths, going for a walk, or practicing mindfulness—the brain begins to create new neural pathways. Over time, the healthier response becomes more automatic, and the brain's reliance on the unhealthy coping mechanism decreases.

Stress and Adaptation: A Double-Edged Sword

While neuroplasticity allows us to adapt to stress, it is crucial to recognize that not all adaptations are beneficial. Chronic exposure to stress can lead to maladaptive changes in the brain. When stress is prolonged or repeated without relief, it can cause the brain to enter a state of hyperactivity, where the stress response becomes overactive. This can result in anxiety, depression, and other mental health challenges. In such cases, the brain has adapted to stress in a way that actually exacerbates the problem.

This is where understanding the role of neuroplasticity becomes critical. It is not enough to simply acknowledge that the brain is adaptable; we must also recognize that adaptation is a double-edged sword. Just as the brain can adapt to unhealthy stress responses, it can also adapt to healthier, more productive ways of coping. The key lies in guiding the brain towards positive adaptations, which can be achieved through mindfulness, cognitive restructuring, and intentional habit change.

For example, one common stress response is rumination—the tendency to dwell on negative thoughts and worries. When we repeatedly engage in rumination, we reinforce neural pathways that perpetuate stress and anxiety. Over time, these pathways become stronger, and it becomes harder to break free from the cycle of negative thinking. However, by practicing mindfulness and focusing on the present moment, we can begin to shift the brain's response to stress. Mindfulness exercises, such as paying attention to breath or engaging in body scans, can help break the cycle of rumination, replacing negative thought patterns with more positive, present-focused ones.

Similarly, cognitive restructuring—challenging negative thought patterns and replacing them with more rational, constructive thoughts—can help rewire the brain's response to adversity. When faced with a stressful situation, we can consciously choose to reframe the challenge in a way that promotes growth, rather than seeing it as an insurmountable obstacle. This shift in perspective has a profound impact on the brain, helping it to adapt in a way that promotes resilience rather than reinforcing the stress response.

Building Resilience Through Neuroplasticity

The ability to build resilience is at the heart of neuroplasticity. Resilience is not a static trait but a dynamic process that can be developed through consistent effort and intentional practice. Just as the brain adapts to stress and adversity, it can also adapt to challenges in ways that enhance our ability to bounce back.

Resilience is cultivated by building new neural pathways that enable us to cope effectively with stress. This process involves strengthening the prefrontal cortex—the area of the brain responsible for emotional regulation, decision-making, and problem-solving. When we practice resilience-building strategies, such as focusing on positive outcomes, practicing gratitude, or developing problem-solving skills, we are actively rewiring the brain to handle stress with greater ease.

Research has shown that engaging in activities that promote emotional regulation, such as mindfulness meditation or physical exercise, can significantly improve brain function and increase resilience. These practices not only help reduce stress but also promote the growth of new neural connections in areas of the brain involved in emotional regulation and resilience. By incorporating these practices into our daily routines, we can strengthen our capacity to handle stress and adversity, ultimately enhancing our ability to thrive in the face of life's challenges.

The Power of Neuroplasticity in Conquering Life's Challenges

In the battle to conquer the struggles of modern life, neuroplasticity is a crucial weapon. The ability to adapt, change, and rewire our brains gives us the power to overcome the challenges that once seemed insurmountable. By harnessing the brain's capacity for growth and transformation, we can reprogram our responses to stress, build new habits, and cultivate resilience in the face of adversity.

The process is not instantaneous—it takes time, patience, and consistent effort. But by understanding the science of neuroplasticity and applying it to our daily lives, we can reshape our minds and ultimately conquer the struggles of modern life.

The Illusion of Control

In the age of constant demands and overwhelming choices, control has become a commodity we all desperately seek. It's a reflex—a reaction to the chaos of modern life. We believe that if we can control the variables around us—our circumstances, our emotions, the people in our lives—we can finally achieve peace and stability. Yet, the harder we try to assert control, the more we often find ourselves in an endless cycle of stress, frustration, and burnout. The reality is that the more we grasp at control, the further it slips from our grasp.

This addiction to control is one of the most insidious struggles of the modern age. It's a deep-seated belief that we can dictate outcomes in every area of life—our careers, relationships, and even our emotional states. But the pursuit of control is an illusion. The more we try to command the uncontrollable, the more we find ourselves powerless.

The key to breaking free from this cycle of anxiety and frustration lies in understanding why we crave control in the first place and, more importantly, why letting go of that illusion may be the antidote to many of the modern struggles we face.

The Roots of the Control Addiction

At its core, our addiction to control stems from fear. Fear of the unknown, fear of failure, and fear of uncertainty. Control offers us a sense of safety, a belief that we can predict and manage the outcomes of our lives. It promises security, even when reality does not. When we're confronted with the complexities and unpredictability of the modern world, it feels natural to try and control every aspect of our existence in an effort to feel grounded and competent.

However, the more we chase control, the more we realize how elusive it truly is. We may be able to control some parts of our lives—our routines, our actions, and our immediate environment—but we cannot control everything. Life has a way of throwing curveballs: unexpected events, external forces, other people's actions, and the ever-present uncertainties that come with being alive. The more we try to control these things, the more we experience frustration and exhaustion, feeling as though we are fighting against a tide that will not relent.

Take the example of work stress. Many of us feel an intense desire to control our careers. We think that if we work hard enough, network enough, and plan enough, we can engineer success. Yet despite our best efforts, setbacks occur: we miss promotions, experience workplace conflicts, or face circumstances beyond our control. The pursuit of control in this context leads not to fulfillment, but to stress, burnout, and an ever-deepening sense of inadequacy.

Control, when pursued at all costs, sets us up for disappointment. This addiction to control leaves us constantly grasping for something we cannot hold, and in the process, we lose sight of the things we can actually influence.

The Myth of Total Control

Our culture reinforces the myth of total control. Everywhere we look, we are bombarded with messages that tell us we can take charge of our destiny, that if we just try harder, plan better, or exert more willpower, we will bend the world to our will. Self-help books, motivational speakers, and social media influencers often promote a message that success and happiness are entirely within our control.

However, this narrative is not only unrealistic, but it also leads to a distorted view of the world. We become fixated on outcomes that are often beyond our reach, and we overlook the process that leads to true success. The myth of total control causes us to neglect the power of adaptability, flexibility, and acceptance—qualities that are much more aligned with real-world resilience.

Consider the constant drive for perfection. We are told that if we meticulously plan and control every detail of our lives, we will avoid mistakes and pitfalls. But in reality, perfection is unattainable, and trying to control every aspect of life only serves to increase our anxiety. The constant striving for control makes us miss the beauty of uncertainty, the opportunities for growth that come from imperfection, and the lessons learned from failure.

In our attempt to control everything, we deny ourselves the chance to experience life as it truly is. Instead of embracing uncertainty and imperfection, we become trapped in an illusion of control—one that holds us hostage to unattainable ideals and robs us of our peace.

The Cost of Clinging to Control

While control may feel comforting in the moment, it comes at a high price. The constant effort to impose our will on the world can lead to mental and physical exhaustion. Research has shown that chronic stress, often the result of trying to control the uncontrollable, can have a profound impact on our health. High levels of stress are linked to a variety of conditions, including heart disease, anxiety, depression, and sleep disorders.

This drive for control can also take a toll on our relationships. When we try to control the people around us—whether it's our partners, children, or coworkers—we inadvertently create tension and conflict. People, by nature, resist being controlled. Instead of fostering healthy, cooperative relationships, our attempts at control often lead to resentment and disconnection.

Moreover, the cost of clinging to control is emotional. The tighter we grip, the more fearful we become. We become hyper-vigilant, anticipating the next problem to solve or the next thing to manage. This mindset traps us in a state of perpetual anxiety. We're constantly waiting for the other shoe to drop, for the next thing to fall out of place, and we end up overwhelmed by the very act of trying to keep everything in order.

The result is a paradox: the more we try to control, the more out of control we feel. Our lives become a string of attempts to regain control, but with each attempt, we end up further distanced from the peace and stability we seek.

The Power of Letting Go

To truly conquer the challenges of modern life, we must acknowledge that control is often an illusion. The more we try to control everything, the more we are disconnected from the present moment—the very moment where life happens. Letting go of the need to control is not about giving up or being passive. It's about embracing life as it is, in all its unpredictability and imperfection.

Letting go begins with accepting that there are things beyond our control—external events, other people's actions, and the ebb and flow of life itself. By acknowledging this, we free ourselves from the constant battle to manipulate outcomes. We stop expending energy on what we can't change and, instead, focus on what we can influence: our responses.

When we stop trying to control every variable, we become more present, more resilient, and more open to the flow of life. Instead of rigidly attempting to dictate every move, we learn to adapt, adjust, and respond in ways that are aligned with our true values and desires. We stop fighting against the current and start flowing with it.

This shift in perspective also allows us to reclaim our energy. When we're not constantly trying to manage everything, we have more capacity to focus on the things that truly matter. We have more room for creativity, connection, and meaningful action. Letting go of control opens up space for new possibilities, growth, and greater freedom.

Embracing Uncertainty and Building Resilience

The key to overcoming the modern struggles that plague us is embracing uncertainty. Life will never be entirely predictable, and we will never have control over every aspect of our existence. But by letting go of the need to control, we free ourselves to engage with life more fully and to build resilience in the face of adversity.

When we stop chasing control, we open ourselves up to growth, learning, and adaptation. Rather than fearing change or difficulty, we come to see them as opportunities to evolve. We become less rigid, more flexible, and ultimately more capable of navigating the ups and downs of life with grace.

Resilience is built not by controlling everything around us, but by mastering our ability to respond to the uncontrollable with equanimity. By accepting that some things are beyond our control, we reclaim our power in the areas where we do have influence—our mindset, our actions, and our relationships.

The Freedom in Letting Go

Ultimately, the pursuit of control is not only futile, but it also prevents us from fully experiencing life. The modern struggles we face are not solved by rigidly trying to dictate outcomes, but by embracing uncertainty, cultivating resilience, and letting go of the illusion that we can control everything.

The true freedom comes not in the pursuit of control, but in the release of it. By letting go, we reclaim our peace, our energy, and our ability to respond to life's challenges with strength and wisdom. The battle for control is a battle we cannot win—but the victory lies in the courage to let go and trust in the flow of life.

Self-Sabotage in the Age of Comparison

In the modern world, the tendency to compare ourselves to others has reached unprecedented heights. With the rise of social media platforms, curated lifestyles, and the pervasive "success culture," comparison has become a silent and often insidious force in our lives. It's a comparison that never ends, an ever-present metric by which we measure our worth. And as a result, we are left struggling with feelings of inadequacy, anxiety, and self-doubt. In fact, this relentless cycle of comparison often leads us to self-sabotage, undermining our own potential and hindering our ability to embrace the fullness of who we are.

The allure of comparing ourselves to others is deceptively powerful. On the surface, it seems harmless. It seems like a way to benchmark our own progress, to understand where we stand in the larger narrative of success. But beneath the surface, comparison can be toxic—it distorts our self-perception and robs us of our confidence and authenticity. The more we fixate on how others are doing, the more we diminish our own value. The endless cycle of comparison fosters a deep-seated belief that we are not enough. And it is this belief that becomes the root of our self-sabotaging behaviors.

But it doesn't have to be this way. By understanding the dynamics of comparison and recognizing how it affects our mindset, we can break free from its grip. Reclaiming our sense of self-worth, independent of external benchmarks, is not only possible, it is essential if we are to conquer the struggles of modern life.

The Modern Comparison Trap

At its core, comparison is an evolutionary instinct. It is a survival mechanism, deeply embedded in our psyche. We compare ourselves to others to measure our status in a social group, to assess our place in the hierarchy.

This instinct may have been helpful in prehistoric times, when social standing directly impacted survival. But in today's world, this mechanism often works against us. The modern age has given birth to an insidious form of comparison: the hyper-curated, polished, and often unrealistic depictions of success, happiness, and achievement that we are bombarded with daily.

Social media, in particular, has amplified this comparison culture. Platforms like Instagram, Facebook, LinkedIn, and Twitter create environments where people post carefully curated versions of their lives—highlight reels, showcasing only the best moments, the achievements, and the luxuries. These platforms present a distorted reality, where success is depicted as effortless and perfection is the norm. As a result, we begin to measure our lives against these curated versions of reality, forgetting that what we see online is often far from the truth.

This constant exposure to others' successes, often in areas where we feel we are lacking, leads to feelings of inadequacy. We find ourselves questioning why we haven't achieved the same milestones, why our lives don't look as polished or exciting, or why we aren't progressing as quickly as others. In our attempts to measure up to these ideals, we often fall short, leading to a sense of failure and a diminished sense of self-worth.

But here's the rub: in this comparison culture, the very metrics by which we judge our own success are arbitrary. Success, happiness, and fulfillment are not universal concepts. What one person defines as success might be completely irrelevant to another. And yet, the more we compare ourselves to others, the more we trap ourselves in a cycle of self-doubt and frustration.

The Dangers of the Comparison Mindset

Comparison creates a toxic mindset—a mindset that breeds self-sabotage. When we constantly measure ourselves against others, we forget to honor our own unique journey. We begin to see ourselves through the lens of what others are doing, rather than celebrating our individual progress and achievements. This shift in perspective can lead to a variety of self-sabotaging behaviors.

1. **Perfectionism and Fear of Failure:** Comparison often leads to perfectionism—the belief that anything less than flawless is unacceptable. We look at others and see their successes, their polished personas, and their apparent ease in achieving their goals. We begin

to believe that if we don't do things perfectly, we will fail. This fear of failure holds us back from taking risks, trying new things, and ultimately moving forward.

2. **Procrastination and Paralysis:** When we constantly measure ourselves against others, we can feel overwhelmed by the seeming gap between where we are and where they are. This can lead to procrastination, as we fear that our efforts won't be good enough. We become paralyzed by the need to do everything just right, and in doing so, we end up doing nothing at all. The comparison mindset fosters a cycle of inaction, which further exacerbates feelings of inadequacy.

3. **Imposter Syndrome:** Comparison is a key trigger for imposter syndrome—the feeling that we don't belong or that we are frauds. As we measure ourselves against the success and accomplishments of others, we begin to doubt our own abilities and achievements. We think that we don't deserve success, that we are just pretending, and that it's only a matter of time before others catch on. Imposter syndrome reinforces our feelings of self-doubt and stops us from fully embracing our accomplishments.

4. **Burnout and Overexertion:** In an attempt to catch up to others or outdo them, we push ourselves beyond our limits. We sacrifice our well-being, our mental health, and our happiness in the pursuit of an idealized version of success. This can lead to burnout—physically, mentally, and emotionally. The constant drive to compete and compare leaves us depleted and disconnected from our true selves.

5. **Negative Self-Talk and Low Self-Worth:** Perhaps the most insidious form of self-sabotage that comparison fosters is negative self-talk. We begin to tell ourselves that we're not good enough, that we'll never measure up, and that we're somehow inferior to others. These thoughts feed into a cycle of low self-worth, reinforcing the belief that we're not capable of achieving what we desire. This constant self-criticism becomes a barrier to growth and progress.

Breaking Free from the Comparison Cycle

The first step in overcoming the self-sabotaging effects of comparison is awareness. We must acknowledge that the need to compare ourselves to others is rooted in insecurity, fear, and external pressures. Once we understand this, we can begin to shift our mindset from one of constant competition to one of self-acceptance and personal growth.

Here are several strategies to help break free from the cycle of comparison and reclaim control over our own narrative:

1. **Practice Radical Self-Acceptance:** The foundation for overcoming comparison is self-acceptance. Instead of seeking validation from others or measuring our worth based on external achievements, we must learn to accept ourselves as we are—flaws, imperfections, and all. Recognizing that we are enough, as we are, allows us to free ourselves from the need to compare and compete with others.

2. **Limit Social Media Exposure:** Social media is a breeding ground for comparison. If you find that scrolling through Instagram or Facebook triggers feelings of inadequacy, it may be time to take a break. Reducing your exposure to curated images of success can help reduce the pressure to measure up. Curate your online experience to include content that uplifts and inspires you, rather than feeds into comparison.

3. **Focus on Your Own Journey:** Instead of comparing your progress to others, focus on your own path. Celebrate the small victories, the incremental growth, and the steps you've taken toward your goals. Recognize that everyone's journey is different, and that where you are now is exactly where you need to be. Comparing your behind-the-scenes to someone else's highlight reel is not a fair or accurate assessment.

4. **Cultivate Gratitude:** Gratitude is a powerful antidote to comparison. When we focus on what we have and express appreciation for our achievements, we shift our mindset from scarcity to abundance. Practicing gratitude helps us to recognize the value in our own lives, regardless of where others stand.

5. **Embrace Imperfection:** Perfection is not only unattainable, but it is also unnecessary. Life is about progress, not perfection. Embrace the beauty of imperfection and give yourself permission to fail, learn, and grow. By letting go of the need for perfection, you free yourself from

the constant cycle of comparison.

6. **Redefine Success:** Success is not a one-size-fits-all concept. What success looks like for someone else may not be the same for you. Take the time to define what success means to you—whether it's fulfillment in your work, joy in your relationships, or personal growth. By redefining success on your own terms, you create a path that is uniquely yours, free from the comparisons that often cloud your judgment.

Embracing Your Own Uniqueness

The culture of comparison is one of the most damaging forces in modern life. It leads to self-sabotage, anxiety, and a distorted sense of self-worth. But by recognizing the illusion of comparison, we can break free from its grip. Instead of measuring our worth against others, we can begin to embrace our own journey, celebrate our progress, and define success on our own terms. In doing so, we free ourselves from the cycle of comparison and move toward a life of self-acceptance, fulfillment, and true success.

Rewriting Your Personal Narrative

The stories we tell ourselves are the threads that weave the fabric of our reality. These narratives, whether consciously or unconsciously constructed, shape how we view the world, ourselves, and our potential. They dictate the choices we make, the actions we take, and the way we respond to adversity. In essence, our personal narratives govern our lives.

But what if these stories are holding us back? What if the narratives we have been telling ourselves are steeped in limiting beliefs, self-doubt, and victimhood? For many, the personal story has become one of struggle, of inability, and of failure. We repeat these stories in our minds, day after day, without realizing how deeply they influence our experiences. And over time, this becomes our truth—the story we live, the reality we create.

Yet, it doesn't have to be this way. The good news is that our personal narrative is not fixed. We have the power to rewrite it. By consciously shaping the stories we tell ourselves, we can change the course of our lives. The ability to rewrite our narrative is the key to reclaiming our power, to breaking free from the constraints of the past, and to taking charge of our future.

The Power of Personal Narratives

We all have a personal story, a narrative that we carry with us from childhood into adulthood. These stories often begin with early experiences—events that shaped our understanding of the world and ourselves. However, not all of these stories are empowering. For many, the story they tell themselves is one of limitation—an identity forged from the mistakes of the past, the judgments of others, or the failures they've experienced.

Consider the story of someone who has struggled with academic failure in school. They may internalize this experience, believing themselves to be "bad at learning" or "not intelligent enough." This story, although rooted in past experiences, continues to shape their behavior and decisions as an adult. Every new challenge is viewed through the lens of this narrative, reinforcing their sense of inadequacy and reinforcing the cycle of failure. The story they tell themselves becomes their reality, shaping their future opportunities and outcomes.

But here's the truth: these stories are not set in stone. The past may have shaped us, but it does not define us. The personal narrative we carry can be altered, reframed, and rewritten. Just as we can change the way we perceive the world, we can change the way we perceive ourselves and our potential.

Understanding the Stories We Tell Ourselves

Before we can rewrite our personal narrative, it's essential to first understand the stories we have been telling ourselves. These narratives often emerge from our past experiences, the messages we received from others, and the societal expectations we internalized. They shape our beliefs about who we are and what we are capable of.

However, the danger lies in identifying too strongly with these stories. We may begin to see ourselves only through the lens of past failures, missed opportunities, or societal judgments. For example, someone who has struggled with weight issues may carry a narrative of "I'm always going to be overweight," or "I'll never have the discipline to stick to a healthy routine." Similarly, someone who has been through a difficult relationship may adopt a story of "I'm not worthy of love" or "I'll never find someone who accepts me for who I am."

These stories are powerful because they dictate our mindset. They determine how we approach new challenges, how we respond to setbacks, and how we perceive our self-worth. The more we hold on to these limiting narratives, the more they shape our reality, trapping us in a cycle of negativity and self-sabotage.

The Illusion of Fixed Identity

One of the most damaging aspects of a fixed personal narrative is the belief in a fixed identity. We often fall into the trap of thinking that the person we were in the past is the person we will always be. We define ourselves by past actions, mistakes, and circumstances, and we convince ourselves that this defines who we are.

But identity is not fixed. It is fluid, dynamic, and ever-evolving. The belief that we are defined by our past is an illusion. Our past does not have to dictate our future. The choices we make in the present moment shape our identity, and the narrative we construct today will lay the foundation for who we become tomorrow.

Rewriting our personal narrative is about letting go of the story that says, "This is who I am and always will be," and embracing the idea that we are constantly in the process of becoming. This mindset shift opens up a world of possibilities, as we realize that we are not bound by our past but empowered to create a future that aligns with our deepest desires.

The Process of Rewriting Your Narrative

Rewriting your personal narrative requires intentional effort, self-awareness, and a willingness to confront your own limiting beliefs. It is not a process of denial or avoidance; it is a process of reclaiming your power and choosing a new path forward. Here's how you can begin the journey of rewriting your personal narrative:

1. Acknowledge the Old Story

The first step in rewriting your narrative is acknowledging the story you've been telling yourself. It's important to recognize the limitations that your current narrative places on you. Ask yourself: What beliefs do I hold about myself that are no longer serving me? What past experiences am I still carrying with me that are holding me back? What are the recurring themes in my life that I wish to change?

By identifying these patterns, you begin to separate the old story from your present reality. You can start to see the ways in which this narrative has limited you and kept you stuck in a cycle of negative thinking. Awareness is the first step toward change.

2. Challenge the Old Beliefs

Once you've identified the limiting beliefs that are tied to your old narrative, it's time to challenge them. Ask yourself: Are these beliefs based on facts, or are they assumptions? What evidence do I have that supports this belief, and what evidence contradicts it?

Many of the beliefs we carry are based on distorted perceptions or outdated information. For example, if you have the belief that you are "not good enough" because of a failure in the past, take the time to objectively assess the situation.

What did you learn from that experience? How did you grow from it? Chances are, the belief that you are "not good enough" is not rooted in the reality of your current capabilities.

3. Reframe the Narrative

Reframing is the process of rewriting your old story into a new, empowering one. Instead of focusing on what you lack or what you failed to achieve, focus on your strengths, your progress, and your potential. Shift the narrative from one of limitation to one of possibility.

For instance, if your old narrative was one of failure, you could reframe it as a story of resilience and learning. Rather than seeing a past mistake as a reflection of your abilities, see it as an opportunity for growth. Every challenge you face can become a chapter in your new story of triumph.

4. Create a Vision for the Future

Rewriting your narrative also involves creating a vision for the future—one that aligns with your deepest desires and values. What kind of person do you want to become? What kind of life do you want to live? Your new narrative should reflect this vision, as it will guide your actions, decisions, and mindset moving forward.

Take time to visualize the future you want to create. Imagine the person you will become when you no longer carry the weight of limiting beliefs. What would it feel like to live with confidence, purpose, and fulfillment? This vision will serve as your guiding star as you continue to rewrite your story.

5. Take Action Aligned with Your New Narrative

Rewriting your personal narrative is not just an intellectual exercise—it requires action. Begin making choices and taking steps that are in alignment with your new narrative. This may mean setting new goals, seeking out new opportunities, or making different decisions than you have in the past. As you take action, you reinforce the new story you are telling yourself and build the life that reflects it.

The Freedom of a Rewritten Narrative

Rewriting your personal narrative is one of the most empowering acts you can undertake. By shifting the story you tell yourself, you free yourself from the constraints of your past and step into a future filled with possibility. Your narrative is not just a reflection of who you were; it is a map of who you are becoming.

As you begin to take control of your narrative, you'll find that your sense of self-worth, your confidence, and your ability to navigate life's challenges grow exponentially. You will begin to see yourself not as a victim of circumstance, but as the author of your own life. And in doing so, you'll reclaim the power that is rightfully yours.

Chapter 3: The Conquering – Taking Action and Building Resilience

The Art of Micro-Conquests

Conquering life's struggles isn't always about dramatic, sweeping victories. It isn't about waiting for that one perfect moment when you can suddenly surge forward, achieving everything in a single, flawless effort. Instead, real progress often happens in the form of small, almost imperceptible steps, taken consistently over time. This approach—what we can call "micro-conquests"—offers a more sustainable, less daunting path toward overcoming the obstacles we face.

The phrase *Veni, Vidi, Vici*—I came, I saw, I conquered—has often been misinterpreted as a statement of singular, grand victories. It conjures images of a warrior returning from battle, chest swollen with pride, holding aloft a trophy of immense value. But what if we could shift our thinking? What if, instead of one monumental conquest, the true path to victory in modern life lay in the accumulation of smaller, manageable wins that slowly add up to something greater?

The Power of Small Wins

The power of micro-conquests is not in their size but in their consistency. It's the daily action, the small decisions that you make every hour, every day, that build momentum and create lasting change. These small wins are the equivalent of laying one brick at a time to build a foundation strong enough to support your entire future.

Take, for instance, the challenge of improving your physical health. The goal of running a marathon can feel overwhelming if you think of it as one massive leap, especially if you're someone who is new to exercise or hasn't been active for years. But if you break it down into smaller, achievable steps—say, walking 10 minutes a day, then gradually increasing your time to 15 minutes, then 20 minutes, and eventually jogging—you begin to experience a series of small victories. Each day that you manage to put on your shoes and walk out the door, you've conquered something. Each small step becomes a conquest, a reminder that you are capable of overcoming what you once thought impossible.

Research on habit formation underscores this principle. In his book *Atomic Habits*, James Clear emphasizes the importance of small, incremental actions. He argues that habits don't have to be grand to be effective. Rather, by focusing on making a 1% improvement each day, the compounded effect of those tiny adjustments can create remarkable change over time. This is the essence of micro-conquests: the recognition that you can achieve your biggest goals not through one giant leap, but through consistent, incremental wins.

The Neuroscience of Small Wins

There is also science backing the power of small victories. When we experience success, our brains release dopamine, a neurotransmitter associated with feelings of pleasure and satisfaction. This release reinforces the behavior that led to success, which in turn motivates us to keep going. However, achieving large, daunting goals can often lead to feelings of anxiety or stress, as the outcome seems too far off or the challenge too overwhelming. In contrast, micro-conquests offer frequent moments of dopamine release, keeping us motivated and reinforcing our commitment to the task at hand.

Small victories also create a feedback loop. When we experience success, even on a minor scale, it boosts our confidence and reinforces our sense of self-efficacy—the belief that we are capable of achieving what we set out to do. This growing sense of competence makes it easier to continue pushing forward, even when the larger goal still feels distant.

Micro-Conquests in Daily Life

This principle of micro-conquests can be applied to virtually any area of life—mental health, productivity, personal development, relationships, and more. Take, for example, the challenge of improving your mental health. The battle against depression, anxiety, or chronic stress can feel insurmountable. The desire to be "better" can feel like an impossible task. But what if the first step was simply committing to a daily act of self-care? A five-minute meditation session, journaling for clarity, or even just taking a few moments to breathe deeply and center yourself. Over time, these small practices can accumulate into a powerful shift in mindset, and your ability to manage stress or negative emotions improves steadily.

It's also true in our professional lives. Instead of tackling an overwhelming to-do list all at once, focusing on knocking off one task at a time, celebrating each completion, can prevent burnout. Micro-conquests in the workplace might include reaching out to one person for collaboration, writing just one page of a report, or making a single decision that moves a project forward. Each small win builds confidence and momentum, allowing us to feel more in control and capable of taking on bigger challenges.

Celebrating Small Victories

One of the most important aspects of micro-conquests is the practice of celebration. It's easy to overlook the small wins, dismissing them as insignificant in the grand scheme of things. However, celebrating each one reinforces the progress you're making and helps to keep your motivation high.

Taking a moment to acknowledge a small success—whether it's as simple as enjoying a cup of coffee after finishing a task, giving yourself a well-deserved break, or treating yourself to something small after completing a goal—helps to solidify the positive feedback loop in your brain. Over time, this positive reinforcement helps to build a stronger, more resilient mindset, one that understands the value of persistence over perfection.

Shifting the Focus from Big Wins to Process

By focusing on micro-conquests, you begin to shift the way you perceive success. The key to overcoming modern struggles is not in the search for the next big achievement but in the daily process of growth. By appreciating the process of growth, you learn to let go of the myth that success comes only through dramatic triumphs. Instead, you can find fulfillment in the journey, recognizing that each step is part of a larger, ongoing victory.

This mindset shift is crucial in today's fast-paced, outcome-driven society. We are constantly bombarded with images of success—whether on social media, in the workplace, or through the lens of public figures. These images can create unrealistic expectations, causing us to feel inadequate when we inevitably fall short of perfection. But micro-conquests challenge that narrative. They teach us that the path to success is not linear, and that it's okay to celebrate the process, not just the destination.

Overcoming the Fear of Failure

One of the most paralyzing obstacles to overcoming modern struggles is the fear of failure. When we think about conquering the challenges of life, the looming shadow of failure often clouds our confidence. The idea of failing, especially in a grand way, can make us hesitant to even begin the journey. Micro-conquests, however, take the pressure off. They allow us to start small, with little to lose, but with much to gain. And in that space, failure becomes less of a threat and more of a learning experience.

Instead of seeing failure as a devastating blow, we can reframe it as part of the process of growth. Each small failure is a stepping stone to greater understanding and success. The key is to keep moving forward, one small victory at a time, without letting the fear of failure stifle our efforts.

The Path to Resilience

Ultimately, micro-conquests are about building resilience. By accumulating small wins, we fortify our minds and spirits, making us more capable of handling setbacks when they inevitably occur. The daily practice of overcoming small challenges teaches us to persevere, to bounce back from adversity, and to keep going even when the road ahead seems long and difficult.

In the same way that a muscle grows stronger through repeated exercise, your resilience grows stronger with each micro-conquest. Over time, this accumulation of small victories creates a robust foundation that allows you to face even larger challenges with confidence and poise.

The Myth of the Lone Hero

Throughout history, the archetype of the lone hero has been romanticized in literature, film, and even in the lives of many successful individuals. From ancient warriors like Achilles and Hector to modern-day figures such as Steve Jobs or Elon Musk, the image of the solitary figure conquering immense odds alone has inspired millions. The myth of the lone hero has become so ingrained in our collective psyche that we often forget the crucial, yet unseen, role of collaboration, support networks, and vulnerability in achieving true success. It is easy to assume that victory is only possible through solitary effort, that real triumph can only come to those who brave their personal battles in isolation. But this view is not only limiting—it is fundamentally flawed.

In modern life, the notion of doing it alone is not just unrealistic, but dangerous. Our struggles today—mental health crises, professional burnout, social pressures—are deeply interconnected with the structures of society around us. No one can truly conquer life's challenges by relying solely on their own strength or vision. To build resilience and experience lasting success, we must first dismantle the myth of the lone hero. This myth creates an illusion of invulnerability, perpetuating the idea that asking for help, showing weakness, or depending on others for support is a form of failure. But in reality, these actions are key to achieving true strength and success.

The Origins of the Lone Hero Myth

The myth of the lone hero traces back to ancient cultures, where warriors, kings, and philosophers were often depicted as solitary figures who faced overwhelming odds alone. Consider the myth of Hercules, whose twelve labors were not just tasks but epic struggles that he allegedly completed through his own strength and cunning. These stories shaped the idea that personal greatness required singular, unassisted feats of courage. Even in the Christian tradition, the image of Jesus' solitary suffering on the cross has left an indelible mark on how we perceive individual struggle.

Over time, this myth evolved into the ideal of the "self-made" man or woman, a person who rises from humble beginnings through sheer grit and determination. The Industrial Revolution and the rise of capitalism further entrenched this narrative, as entrepreneurs and innovators were glorified as individuals who created monumental change through their own efforts. From the stories of Henry Ford to the tech giants of Silicon Valley, the lone visionary persevering against the odds has become a dominant figure in modern culture.

But in today's interconnected world, this myth does a disservice to our understanding of success. The pressure to "do it alone" not only breeds isolation but also fosters unrealistic expectations of perfection. In reality, the ability to reach out for help, to collaborate, and to lean on a network of supportive relationships is essential to overcoming the challenges of modern life.

Collaboration: The Key to Resilience

Resilience, contrary to popular belief, is not about going it alone when things get tough. It is about building a network of support, seeking guidance when necessary, and sharing the burden of stress, frustration, and uncertainty. There is power in collective strength, and resilience often arises not from solitary effort but from the collective response to adversity.

One of the most profound shifts we can make in our pursuit of victory is to recognize that collaboration is not a sign of weakness—it is a strategic move that strengthens our chances for long-term success. This is particularly relevant in our current age, where the complexity of modern challenges often requires interdisciplinary knowledge and skills. No individual, no matter how brilliant, can effectively navigate the intricacies of today's world alone.

Let's take the example of startups and entrepreneurial ventures. While many tech founders, like Steve Jobs or Mark Zuckerberg, are often celebrated for their visionary leadership, they did not succeed in isolation. Behind every major company is a network of collaborators, investors, advisors, and team members who play an instrumental role in bringing the founder's vision to life. Even more importantly, these individuals often act as emotional and psychological support systems for the founder, helping them overcome the inevitable setbacks and obstacles that arise along the way.

The myth of the lone hero also neglects the power of mentorship and coaching. Whether it's in the context of business, personal development, or mental health, the guidance of others can dramatically accelerate our progress. Many of the most successful people in the world owe part of their success to the mentors who helped shape their mindset and provided crucial advice during times of doubt. Seeking mentorship or guidance is not a sign of inadequacy but a strategic decision to learn from others and build upon their wisdom.

Vulnerability: The Strength in Asking for Help

A core element of the lone hero myth is the idea that vulnerability is to be avoided at all costs. To be vulnerable is often seen as a weakness in a world that prizes strength, control, and independence. However, it is exactly through vulnerability that we can unlock deeper resilience.

In the context of mental health, vulnerability is a cornerstone of true strength. Opening up about our struggles, whether to a therapist, a friend, or a support group, is often the first step in overcoming them. Research shows that those who seek help when facing emotional or psychological difficulties tend to recover more quickly and with more long-term success than those who keep their struggles hidden. This is because vulnerability fosters connection and trust, both of which are essential for resilience.

In a world that demands we "show up strong" at all times, it takes real courage to admit when we are struggling. But it is this courage to ask for help, to lean on others when we need it most, that ultimately builds the resilience needed to conquer life's challenges.

Consider the example of athletes at the top of their game. While they often seem invincible on the field, many of the world's best athletes rely heavily on coaches, nutritionists, psychologists, and support staff to stay at the top of their sport. They understand that it is not just physical strength but a network of support that helps them overcome challenges, improve performance, and recover from setbacks. By accepting their vulnerabilities and working with a team, they enhance their resilience.

In the workplace, a similar phenomenon occurs. While many successful leaders present an image of calm confidence, behind the scenes, they often rely on trusted colleagues, team members, and mentors to navigate challenges. The ability to ask for help, delegate tasks, and rely on others' expertise is not a weakness; it is a strategic move that amplifies the leader's ability to succeed.

Successful leaders, in fact, are often the best at knowing when to lean on their teams and build a network of experts who can support their vision.

The Role of Community in Building Resilience

Our greatest victories, whether personal or professional, are often achieved through community efforts. There is strength in numbers, and when we come together, we are capable of overcoming even the most daunting challenges. This concept is particularly important when dealing with personal battles, such as mental health struggles or the challenges of burnout.

Communities offer a sense of belonging and emotional support that cannot be replicated by solitary efforts. They provide a space for vulnerability and understanding, where individuals can share their struggles and gain strength from others who have faced similar challenges. The act of sharing, whether through social support groups, online communities, or close personal relationships, helps reduce the stigma surrounding struggle and allows for collective healing.

Take, for instance, the global movement surrounding mental health awareness. As more individuals come forward to share their experiences, it has become increasingly clear that mental health is not a battle fought in isolation. Many people have found strength in the support of others who understand their pain, and in turn, these shared experiences have paved the way for greater acceptance, understanding, and healing.

In addition, when we acknowledge the importance of collaboration, we begin to recognize the inherent value in the diverse perspectives and experiences of others. This approach is fundamental in overcoming the challenges of modern life. The problems we face today—whether technological addiction, burnout, or anxiety—are often complex and multifaceted. No single person has the answers, but by coming together and sharing ideas, we are better equipped to solve them.

Moving Beyond the Myth

To truly conquer life's challenges, we must shift our mindset from one of solitary struggle to one of collective strength. This shift requires us to embrace collaboration, to actively seek out mentors, and to lean into vulnerability. We must acknowledge that strength lies not in going it alone but in forging meaningful relationships, both personal and professional, that can help support us when the going gets tough.

Victory, as the myth of the lone hero suggests, is not about individual achievement. It is about the strength of a collective effort, the wisdom of shared experience, and the power of community. As we move forward in our own battles, we must remember that it is through collaboration, vulnerability, and community that we will find the true resilience necessary to conquer the struggles of modern life.

By letting go of the myth of the lone hero, we open ourselves to the real possibility of triumph—one that is shared with others, built upon collective strength, and rooted in the deep connections we form with those around us.

Hacking Your Habit Loop

As we step into the realm of conquering our modern struggles, one fundamental truth stands out: the real battle is not always external. Often, the most daunting challenge we face is the fight within ourselves—the daily grind of managing our habits, our routines, and our tendencies. It is in our habits that the power to either transform or stagnate lies. Understanding and mastering the mechanics of habit formation is one of the most effective ways to gain control over our lives and ultimately conquer the battles that seem insurmountable.

In this subchapter, we will delve into the science of habits—how they are formed, how they govern our lives, and how we can use this knowledge to craft new, empowering routines that align with our goals. The concept of "hacking" your habit loop isn't about tricking your brain into following a shortcut, but rather about understanding how habits are wired in the brain and reprogramming them to work for you, not against you.

The Neuroscience of Habit Formation

At its core, a habit is a loop—a cycle of behavior that repeats automatically and requires little conscious thought. This loop is composed of three parts: the **cue**, the **routine**, and the **reward**. Understanding these components and how they interact with one another is key to altering your habits.

1. **Cue (Trigger):** Every habit starts with a cue. This is the signal or prompt that triggers the habitual behavior. It can be external (e.g., seeing a notification on your phone) or internal (e.g., feeling stressed, hungry, or bored). The cue doesn't have to be something significant; it can be as simple as a thought, an emotion, or a specific environment.

2. **Routine (Behavior):** The routine is the action or behavior that follows the cue. This is the habit itself—the thing you do automatically

in response to the trigger. It might be checking social media, going for a run, or even something like procrastinating when you feel overwhelmed.

3. **Reward:** After completing the routine, your brain experiences a reward—a positive feeling or a sense of satisfaction. This is what reinforces the habit loop. The reward doesn't have to be grand, but it needs to be something that your brain perceives as beneficial, even if just for a moment. This is why bad habits like eating junk food or procrastinating are so hard to break: the reward is immediate, even if it's ultimately detrimental in the long term.

The problem with habits isn't that they exist; it's that many of them are formed unconsciously. Our brain's desire for efficiency leads us to repeat behaviors that seem to offer rewards, even when they're harmful or misaligned with our values. However, this same mechanism also gives us the power to rewire our habits with intentionality and purpose.

The Power of Keystone Habits

One of the most powerful tools in hacking your habit loop is the concept of **keystone habits**. These are habits that have a ripple effect on other areas of your life. When you adopt a keystone habit, it doesn't just improve that one aspect of your life—it often leads to a cascade of positive changes in other areas as well.

For instance, regular physical exercise is a keystone habit. It doesn't just improve your fitness; it can also enhance your mental health, boost productivity, improve your sleep, and foster better eating habits. Once the habit of exercising regularly is in place, it often leads to a cascade of other beneficial habits, such as preparing healthier meals, practicing mindfulness, and setting aside time for rest.

Another example of a keystone habit might be journaling. Taking five minutes a day to reflect on your thoughts and emotions doesn't just help you process feelings; it can lead to greater self-awareness, better decision-making, and improved relationships. By focusing on these high-leverage habits, you're essentially setting up a foundation for broader change.

By focusing on just a few key habits, you can rapidly shift your life trajectory. But the key to success lies in the process of habit stacking—connecting new habits to existing routines, making them easier to integrate into your life. For example, if you already have the habit of drinking coffee in the morning, you could pair it with a short morning meditation or planning session. By making the new habit an extension of an already established one, you increase the chances of sticking with it.

The Importance of Small Wins: Micro-Habits

When it comes to hacking your habit loop, the focus should be on **micro-habits**—tiny, manageable actions that build momentum over time. Micro-habits are smaller than goals; they are the smallest possible action you can take toward creating a new habit. The beauty of micro-habits lies in their simplicity. They don't require massive willpower, and they don't take up much time. However, over time, their cumulative impact can be profound.

For instance, instead of committing to an hour of exercise every day, you could start with just two minutes. This tiny commitment is not overwhelming, yet it plants the seed for building a larger exercise routine. Over time, you will begin to crave the reward—whether it's the endorphin boost or the feeling of accomplishment—that comes with your micro-habit. Eventually, that two-minute session can expand into longer workouts as the behavior becomes ingrained.

This concept aligns with what researchers call the **power of consistency**. In a world that prizes grand gestures and dramatic transformations, it's easy to overlook the significance of small, incremental steps. But it's these small, consistent actions that lead to big changes. This is the essence of conquering modern life's challenges: creating a momentum that propels you forward with minimal effort.

The Role of Environment in Habit Formation

We are, to a large extent, products of our environment. Our surroundings have a profound impact on the habits we form, both positively and negatively. When you're attempting to alter a habit, it's crucial to design your environment in such a way that it supports your goals.

For example, if you want to eat healthier, make it easier for yourself by placing nutritious foods within reach and removing junk food from your home. If you're trying to build a writing habit, create a designated writing space that is free from distractions. If you want to read more, leave books in areas where you're likely to pick them up, such as next to your bed or on your desk.

The process of habit formation can be greatly enhanced by eliminating friction. The more difficult it is to perform an undesirable behavior, the less likely you are to engage in it. Conversely, the easier you make it to engage in your desired behavior, the more likely it is to stick. This principle can be applied to every area of your life: work, health, relationships, and more.

Furthermore, accountability plays a crucial role in shaping habits. When we share our goals with others, we create a form of social pressure that reinforces our commitment. This could be a workout buddy, a friend who checks in on your progress, or an online community where you share updates. The sense of responsibility that comes with accountability helps solidify your habits and makes it easier to push through when motivation wanes.

The Power of Self-Compassion in Habit Change

One of the greatest barriers to successfully hacking your habit loop is the tendency to be overly harsh with ourselves when we slip up. Breaking a bad habit or starting a new one is rarely a smooth path; there are bumps along the way, and setbacks are inevitable. However, how we respond to those setbacks can make or break our progress.

Self-compassion is a critical tool in the habit change process. When we view our failures as part of the learning process, rather than as signs of our inadequacy, we're more likely to persist. Research in psychology has shown that people who practice self-compassion are more resilient when it comes to making lasting changes. Instead of berating ourselves for missing a workout or eating junk food, we can acknowledge the slip-up, learn from it, and move forward with renewed commitment.

Building a Sustainable Habit Loop for Conquest

Hacking your habit loop is not about finding shortcuts or quick fixes. It's about understanding the psychology and neuroscience behind your behaviors and leveraging that knowledge to create long-term, sustainable change. By focusing on small wins, identifying keystone habits, designing an environment that supports your goals, and practicing self-compassion, you can build habits that work for you, not against you.

As you embark on the journey of conquering life's struggles, remember that victory is not the result of a singular event—it is the result of consistent, deliberate action. The habits you form today shape your future, and with intentionality and perseverance, you can transform even the most daunting challenges into opportunities for growth. Conquer your habits, and you will conquer your life.

The Resilience Hierarchy

Resilience isn't something you're born with, nor is it a trait that you either possess or lack. Instead, resilience is a skill, an evolving state of mind that can be cultivated, refined, and harnessed over time. In this subchapter, we will introduce a new framework: The Resilience Hierarchy. It's a model that explains how emotional, physical, and mental resilience work together to create a robust defense against the challenges of modern life. It's designed to be more than a theoretical concept—this is a practical structure that you can use to build your own resilience, piece by piece, until it becomes second nature.

The Hierarchy of Resilience: Building Strength from the Ground Up

At its core, the Resilience Hierarchy posits that true resilience is a multi-layered construct. Each layer supports the others, creating a cohesive structure. If one layer falters or is weak, it can have a destabilizing effect on the whole. Just like a building that requires a solid foundation before it can rise to great heights, our resilience must be built from the inside out.

Layer 1: Physical Resilience – The Foundation

Physical resilience is the first layer in the hierarchy. Without a strong physical foundation, the rest of your resilience cannot stand firm. The mind and body are intricately linked, and the state of your body directly impacts your mental and emotional well-being. Physical resilience is more than just endurance or strength; it's about your body's ability to recover from stress, injury, or fatigue. It's about maintaining vitality and health despite the external pressures you face.

1. **Exercise as a Pillar of Physical Resilience:**
   Exercise is one of the most powerful tools to build physical resilience. It doesn't need to be extreme or time-consuming; it simply needs to be consistent. Regular physical activity is proven to lower stress,

reduce anxiety, and improve sleep—all of which contribute to greater emotional and mental resilience. Exercise is also a powerful tool for rewiring your brain. Physical exertion stimulates the release of endorphins, known as the "feel-good" hormones, which can improve your mood and combat negative thinking.

2. **Nutrition and Hydration**:
The food we consume plays a critical role in our physical and mental health. A diet rich in whole foods—fruits, vegetables, lean proteins, and healthy fats—nourishes the body, providing the nutrients it needs to thrive. When we neglect our physical needs, we compromise our ability to handle stress, focus, and recover. Additionally, staying hydrated is essential to maintaining mental clarity and emotional balance. It's easy to overlook the basics, but a proper diet and adequate water intake are the bedrock of all resilience.

3. **Rest and Recovery**:
Physical resilience is not just about exertion; it's also about recovery. The human body requires rest in order to repair and recharge. Sleep is a cornerstone of resilience. During sleep, your body undergoes physical repairs, strengthens the immune system, and processes the emotional weight of the day. Poor sleep disrupts all other aspects of resilience, making you more vulnerable to stress and fatigue.

The first layer of resilience, physical strength, builds the necessary stamina for the battles of life. It ensures that you are not only capable of handling external pressures but also that you can recover quickly and keep moving forward when faced with setbacks.

Layer 2: Emotional Resilience – The Inner Strength

While physical resilience helps you manage the external stresses of life, emotional resilience is the next layer, dealing with your internal world. Emotional resilience refers to your ability to handle life's emotional turbulence—loss, disappointment, stress, and fear—with grace and poise. It's not about avoiding difficult emotions but about navigating them with the knowledge and skills that will allow you to return to a place of balance.

1. **Self-Awareness**:

The first step in developing emotional resilience is self-awareness—the ability to observe and understand your own emotional reactions. Most people go through life on autopilot, unaware of the emotions driving their actions. When you lack self-awareness, you are at the mercy of your emotions. By cultivating the ability to recognize and label your emotions as they arise, you gain the ability to regulate them.

2. **Emotional Regulation**:

Emotional resilience is largely about mastering emotional regulation—the ability to respond to emotions thoughtfully rather than reacting impulsively. Learning to regulate emotions doesn't mean suppressing them, but rather responding in ways that serve your well-being. For example, when faced with frustration or anger, emotional regulation allows you to pause, breathe, and choose a healthier response, such as expressing your feelings constructively or seeking a solution.

3. **Cognitive Reappraisal**:

One of the most powerful tools for emotional resilience is **cognitive reappraisal**—the ability to reframe a situation and find a more constructive interpretation. For instance, when you face a challenging situation, instead of viewing it as a threat, you might reinterpret it as an opportunity for growth. Reappraisal allows you to detach from the emotional weight of a situation and approach it from a more objective perspective, reducing feelings of stress and increasing your ability to problem-solve.

4. **Support Networks**:

Emotional resilience is not just about internal strength; it also involves the external resources you rely on. Human beings are social creatures, and relationships are an essential part of emotional resilience. Surrounding yourself with a support network—friends, family, mentors, or even a therapist—provides you with emotional safety nets when you're facing difficult times. The key here is vulnerability. Emotional resilience grows stronger when you allow yourself to be vulnerable and reach out for support when needed.

The second layer of resilience, emotional strength, ensures that you can face the emotional storms of life without being swept away. It's about developing the flexibility to bend without breaking and the inner resources to heal and recover from emotional wounds.

Layer 3: Mental Resilience – The Power of Mindset

The final layer in the Resilience Hierarchy is mental resilience. While physical and emotional resilience address the body and emotions, mental resilience is the ability to face life's challenges with clarity, focus, and determination. It's about mental fortitude—the strength of mind to push through setbacks, to stay focused on your goals, and to embrace change and uncertainty with confidence.

1. **Growth Mindset**:
   One of the foundational principles of mental resilience is the **growth mindset**—the belief that abilities and intelligence can be developed through effort, learning, and perseverance. This mindset enables you to view challenges as opportunities for growth rather than insurmountable obstacles. When faced with difficulty, someone with a growth mindset believes that through hard work, persistence, and the right strategies, they can improve and eventually overcome any challenge. This mindset empowers you to see setbacks not as failures but as stepping stones on the path to success.

2. **Focus and Attention**:
   Mental resilience is also about focus—the ability to stay present and concentrate on the task at hand, even in the face of distractions. In today's world of constant digital interruptions and multitasking, maintaining focus can feel like a lost art. But mental resilience relies on your ability to block out distractions and commit your energy fully to the present moment. Whether it's staying focused during work, engaging in deep thinking, or simply being present with loved ones, focus is a core element of mental resilience.

3. **Mindfulness and Acceptance**:
   Mindfulness—the practice of paying attention to the present moment without judgment—is another key element of mental resilience. It allows you to accept whatever is happening without resistance, which

in turn reduces the power that stress and worry have over you. When you cultivate mindfulness, you train your mind to approach challenges with curiosity and openness, rather than fear or anxiety. This mindset allows you to embrace the uncertainty of life and face it with calm and clarity.

4. **Purpose and Meaning:**

   The most resilient individuals are those who live with a sense of purpose. Mental resilience is deeply connected to having a clear sense of meaning in life. When you know your "why," when you have a strong sense of purpose, you are better able to weather the storms of life. Purpose gives you the mental fortitude to persevere through challenges because it provides you with direction and motivation. Whether your purpose is professional, personal, or spiritual, it acts as a compass, guiding you toward your goals even in difficult times.

The third layer of resilience, mental strength, provides the clarity and focus needed to navigate life's complexities with confidence. It gives you the determination to keep moving forward, even when the road ahead is uncertain.

The Interdependence of the Layers

Each layer of resilience is interconnected. Physical resilience supports emotional and mental resilience, emotional resilience enhances mental resilience, and mental resilience drives physical action. Together, they form a holistic, self-reinforcing system that can carry you through the toughest times.

It's important to understand that resilience is not a one-time fix—it's an ongoing process. Life will always present challenges, but by continually strengthening the layers of your resilience, you can build an unshakable foundation that enables you to weather any storm.

By working on your physical health, cultivating emotional intelligence, and sharpening your mental focus, you build a resilience that isn't just about surviving—it's about thriving. It's about stepping into the arena of life with the confidence that you can handle whatever comes your way.

In the end, true resilience isn't just about bouncing back; it's about bouncing forward, stronger, more adaptable, and better prepared for whatever challenges lie ahead. As you build your Resilience Hierarchy, you don't just conquer life's struggles—you master the art of living with power and purpose, no matter the circumstances.

The Power of 'No'

In a world that celebrates hustle, perpetual availability, and the endless pursuit of more, the ability to say "no" has become one of the most powerful tools in conquering the struggles of modern life. We live in a culture that glorifies being busy—where every moment must be filled with activity, every second optimized, and every opportunity seized. We say "yes" to commitments, to requests, to ideas, and to people because we fear missing out, disappointing others, or being seen as unproductive or lazy. Yet, it is in the strategic use of "no" that we reclaim our time, our energy, and our mental peace.

Saying "no" is not about being dismissive or refusing help or engagement. It is about conscious, intentional decision-making. It is about having the wisdom to prioritize your most important values, goals, and needs over the demands of the external world. The paradox of saying "no" is that it ultimately allows you to say "yes" to the things that truly matter. This subchapter will explore how learning to wield the power of "no" is an essential step in conquering the chaos of modern life, allowing you to focus on what truly contributes to your well-being, growth, and success.

The Cultural Addiction to "Yes"

Our modern culture is steeped in the expectation of "yes." From the workplace to personal relationships, from social media to family gatherings, saying "yes" has become synonymous with success, responsibility, and social acceptability. We are taught that the more we do, the more valuable we are, the busier we appear, the more productive we must be. We wear busyness like a badge of honor, and any indication that we might slow down or say "no" is often met with guilt or concern from others. The result is an unsustainable pace of life, one that leaves us feeling overwhelmed, distracted, and stretched too thin.

The problem with this "yes" addiction is that it leaves little room for reflection, self-care, or deep engagement with the tasks and people that actually align with our true priorities. Constantly saying "yes" leads to burnout, stress, and a sense of powerlessness over one's time and energy. Ironically, while we might think we are succeeding by constantly adding more to our plates, we are only diluting our effectiveness and diminishing our well-being.

The first step in reclaiming control is recognizing the need to say "no" without guilt or hesitation. By understanding the value of boundaries, we can prioritize our health, personal growth, and happiness over the demands of others.

The Paradox of Less Is More

The art of saying "no" is fundamentally about recognizing that *less is more*. In the modern world, we are overwhelmed by options—be it social engagements, career opportunities, or consumption. The paradox of choice, as we discussed earlier, is a real issue in today's world. With so many opportunities and requests clamoring for our attention, it's easy to feel as though we need to say "yes" to everything to make progress or to stay relevant.

However, by trying to do everything, we ultimately fail to do anything well. Our energies become scattered, our focus diluted, and our ability to truly excel at any one task becomes compromised. Saying "no" to distractions and non-essential tasks allows us to concentrate our efforts where they matter most.

The power of "no" lies in its ability to create space. Space to breathe. Space to think. Space to grow. Space to focus on the projects, relationships, and activities that align with your deeper goals and values. By saying "no" to what doesn't serve you, you automatically say "yes" to your own priorities. In this sense, less is more, because it gives you the ability to do more with what truly matters.

The Strength of Setting Boundaries

Boundaries are the silent architects of resilience. They define the limits of what we are willing to accept, the space in which we are willing to exist, and the ways in which we protect our emotional and physical health. Setting boundaries is not just about saying "no" to others—it is also about saying "no" to ourselves. It's about recognizing when we are overcommitting or pushing ourselves beyond healthy limits.

When you refuse to set boundaries, you allow external demands to dictate the course of your life. The inability to say "no" leaves you at the mercy of every request, every social expectation, every interruption. But when you create and enforce boundaries, you create the conditions for your own success and happiness. Boundaries enable you to protect your time, your energy, and your sense of self. They are an act of self-respect and self-care.

For example, when you set boundaries around your work, you protect your personal time, ensuring that you don't sacrifice your mental and physical health for the sake of productivity. When you set boundaries in relationships, you ensure that your connections remain healthy, respectful, and mutually beneficial rather than draining and toxic. By consistently setting boundaries, you communicate to yourself and others that your time and energy are valuable, and you are willing to protect them at all costs.

Saying "No" as an Act of Prioritization

In the battle for our attention and energy, saying "no" is not just about refusing external demands—it is an act of prioritization. In a world full of distractions, we are forced to choose what we give our time and focus to. If we are always saying "yes" to everything, we are left with no time or resources to pursue our most important goals.

Each time you say "no" to something that doesn't align with your priorities, you create space to say "yes" to something more important. Whether it's dedicating time to a personal project, focusing on your health, or nurturing meaningful relationships, saying "no" gives you the freedom to prioritize what truly matters.

This process of prioritization is one of the most important aspects of conquering the struggles of modern life. When you focus on fewer things but give them your full attention, you cultivate a deeper sense of accomplishment and fulfillment. Success in modern life doesn't come from doing everything; it comes from doing the right things well.

Overcoming the Guilt of Saying "No"

One of the greatest barriers to using the power of "no" is guilt. Many of us were raised to believe that saying "no" is rude, selfish, or disrespectful. We fear that by refusing someone's request, we will disappoint them or damage the relationship. This guilt, however, is often misplaced. The truth is that we cannot pour from an empty cup. If we continually say "yes" to others at the expense of our own well-being, we will eventually burn out and be unable to help anyone, least of all ourselves.

Overcoming the guilt of saying "no" begins with reframing how we view boundaries. Rather than seeing them as rejection, we can view them as acts of self-preservation and acts of respect—for both ourselves and others. When you say "no," you are choosing to prioritize your own needs, which ultimately allows you to show up more fully and more effectively for others when it matters most. Saying "no" isn't about being selfish; it's about being sustainable.

Practical Strategies for Saying "No"

Now that we've explored the importance of saying "no," how can we implement this practice effectively? Here are a few practical strategies for wielding the power of "no" in your daily life:

1. **Be Direct and Polite**: When you need to say "no," be clear, direct, and polite. There is no need for elaborate excuses or justifications. A simple, "I'm sorry, but I can't take this on right now," or "I appreciate the offer, but I need to decline," is sufficient. You don't need to explain yourself in great detail. Keep it short and respectful.

2. **Offer Alternatives**: If you feel comfortable and appropriate, offer alternatives. For example, if a friend asks for your help but you're unable to commit, you might suggest another time or another person who could assist. This helps to maintain goodwill without compromising your own boundaries.

3. **Practice Self-Compassion**: Understand that saying "no" is an act of self-compassion. You are not obligated to do everything for everyone. Being kind to yourself is essential for maintaining your resilience. The more you practice saying "no," the more comfortable and confident you will become in doing so.

4. **Use Time Blocks**: Protect your time by creating dedicated time blocks for work, relaxation, and personal activities. When you know you have a set amount of time for something, it becomes easier to say "no" to requests that fall outside those blocks.

5. **Evaluate Requests**: Before saying "yes" to anything, take a moment to evaluate whether the request aligns with your priorities. If it doesn't, then saying "no" is not just a necessity, but a strategy for ensuring you stay focused on your most important goals.

The Lasting Impact of Saying "No"

Learning to say "no" is one of the most powerful tools you can use to conquer the struggles of modern life. It allows you to take control of your time, your energy, and your mental space. It creates the room necessary for true success and fulfillment.

The more you practice the power of "no," the more you will find that you are not only protecting your well-being but also creating a life that aligns more closely with your values and purpose. Saying "no" is not the end of opportunities—it is the gateway to the right opportunities. It is a tool of discernment, allowing you to cut through the noise and focus on what truly matters.

In the end, the power of "no" is the key to building the resilient mindset and lifestyle that will allow you to conquer modern life's challenges. Through boundaries, prioritization, and strategic refusal, you can create the space necessary for personal growth, fulfillment, and lasting success.

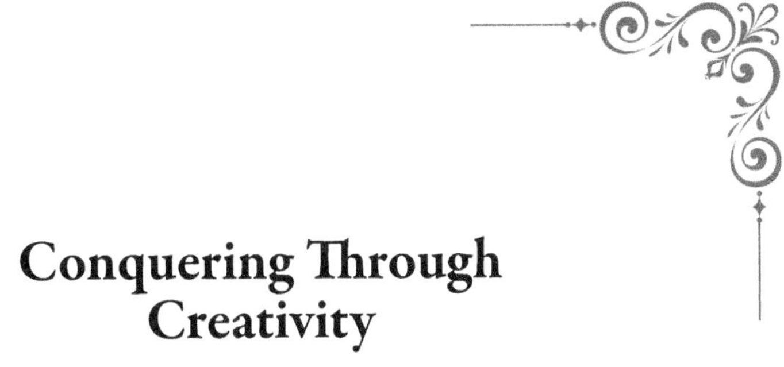

Conquering Through Creativity

In a world where stress and conflict seem ever-present, finding healthy outlets to navigate and resolve these challenges has become more important than ever. For many, the answer lies not in sheer force or willpower, but in creativity. Creativity offers a unique way of confronting life's struggles—whether emotional, mental, or even physical—by providing a means to transform obstacles into opportunities for growth, expression, and healing. This subchapter explores how harnessing the power of creativity can become a central strategy in conquering modern life's battles.

At first glance, creativity may seem unrelated to personal resilience. After all, how can something as abstract as artistic expression or problem-solving help in the face of overwhelming stress, burnout, or emotional turmoil? The truth, however, is that creativity is not just confined to the arts; it is a mindset, a tool that can be applied to every aspect of life. It allows us to reframe challenges, to innovate, and to adapt. Creativity helps us look at problems from different angles, find new solutions, and give meaning to our struggles.

In this subchapter, we will explore the profound connection between creativity and resilience, how to use creative outlets for stress relief and conflict resolution, and how innovation and artistic expression can reshape your challenges. Creativity isn't just a way to deal with life's pressures; it's a way to thrive amidst them.

The Link Between Creativity and Resilience

Resilience is often understood as the ability to bounce back from adversity. But it's more than just recovering—it's about adapting and growing stronger through the process. Creativity is a vital part of this growth because it encourages adaptability. When faced with a challenge, the creative mind doesn't simply look for the quickest solution. It explores alternatives, considers various perspectives, and finds innovative ways to overcome obstacles. By tapping into creativity, we are better equipped to deal with stress and setbacks by seeing them not as permanent roadblocks but as opportunities for transformation.

For example, imagine you are overwhelmed with the pressures of work and personal life. The immediate response might be to retreat into anxiety or frustration. But if you approach this stress creatively—whether through brainstorming solutions, journaling your thoughts, or even making art—you open up a space for new ideas and fresh perspectives. Creativity encourages you to explore the problem from multiple angles, which allows you to come up with solutions that would otherwise remain hidden in the heat of the moment.

In fact, creativity can help you reframe adversity itself. When we face challenges, we often see them as threats. Yet, in the creative process, challenges are often viewed as material—something to be shaped, transformed, and molded. The very act of transforming a problem into an artistic project, for instance, can diminish its hold on you, turning something painful into something beautiful or at least manageable.

Stress Relief Through Creative Outlets

One of the most direct ways creativity helps us conquer modern life's struggles is by providing a healthy outlet for stress. Stress manifests physically, emotionally, and mentally. Chronic stress can take a toll on our body's immune system, our mental clarity, and even our relationships. The importance of finding a way to release stress in a healthy manner cannot be overstated. Creativity offers a channel to do just that.

Artistic activities like painting, writing, playing music, or dancing allow the mind to focus on something outside of the immediate stressor, providing a break from negative thought patterns. These activities are more than just a distraction—they activate the brain's reward system, releasing dopamine and other feel-good chemicals. Whether you are creating something tangible, like a piece of art, or engaging in a performance, the act itself helps soothe the nervous system, calm anxiety, and restore balance to the mind and body.

For instance, painting can be incredibly therapeutic. The act of blending colors, applying brushstrokes, or simply observing the flow of paint on canvas creates a meditative experience. You are forced to be present in the moment, a practice that counters the fast-paced, hyperconnected world we live in. Even if the end result isn't a masterpiece, the process itself can provide relief from the stress you carry. Similarly, writing about your emotions, whether through poetry, journaling, or storytelling, can help untangle complex feelings and provide clarity.

Moreover, creative outlets allow for a level of emotional expression that words alone may not achieve. Many people struggle to communicate their innermost thoughts and feelings, especially when dealing with difficult emotions like sadness, anger, or frustration. In such moments, creativity allows us to express what words cannot—sometimes the act of creation is enough to release pent-up emotions.

Innovation as a Tool for Problem Solving

Creativity is not just about creating art or finding ways to release stress; it is also a tool for solving problems. Modern life is full of complex challenges that require innovative solutions. By cultivating creativity, we can tap into a well of resources that allow us to face difficulties with more ingenuity and resourcefulness.

Think of the last time you faced a significant challenge—whether it was at work, in a relationship, or within yourself. The solution may not have been immediately apparent. In these moments, our usual problem-solving mechanisms—logical thinking, systematic approaches—might fail us because the issue at hand is too complicated or too overwhelming. Creativity allows us to think outside the box and find new solutions. Rather than getting stuck in frustration, a creative mindset encourages us to experiment, to take risks, and to try new approaches.

For example, if you find yourself in a deadlock with a colleague, instead of adhering to the usual strategies of negotiation or conflict resolution, why not try a creative approach? Could you solve the problem through a new form of collaboration, or perhaps frame the issue differently? Could you use humor, or tap into shared passions, to create a bridge to understanding? Creative solutions allow you to reimagine the scenario and move past barriers that would otherwise be insurmountable.

Moreover, creativity can be especially powerful when it comes to reimagining setbacks and failures. In modern life, we often see failure as the end of the road, but the creative process thrives on experimentation, which involves trial and error. When we embrace creativity, we allow ourselves to fail productively—meaning we learn, adapt, and grow from each failure.

Using Creative Practices for Conflict Resolution

Conflict is inevitable in every aspect of life, but how we respond to it can define whether we emerge stronger or more stressed. Creativity plays a powerful role in resolving conflict—both internally and externally. Rather than defaulting to aggression, avoidance, or passive-aggressiveness, creativity provides alternative ways of approaching disputes.

In personal relationships, for example, creativity can help us find new ways to communicate, de-escalate tension, and reconnect with others. Writing a letter to express feelings, engaging in a creative activity together (such as cooking or painting), or even using metaphor and storytelling to explain one's emotions can help resolve conflicts without resorting to confrontation.

Similarly, creativity can provide internal conflict resolution. When we face mental turmoil, anxiety, or self-doubt, creative expression can offer a pathway to self-understanding. Rather than suppressing these feelings or allowing them to overwhelm us, we can channel them into creative outlets. This allows us to externalize the conflict, which makes it easier to resolve.

Another aspect of creative conflict resolution involves reframing the conflict itself. When you approach a problem creatively, you can reinterpret it in a way that aligns with your values or deeper goals. For example, what if you viewed a stressful project at work as an opportunity to learn a new skill or as a challenge to push your limits? This shift in perspective—encouraged by creativity—helps alleviate the pressure that comes with conflict.

Building a Resilient Mindset Through Creative Exploration

Finally, creativity is an essential tool in building a resilient mindset. Resilience doesn't just come from overcoming adversity—it comes from constantly adapting and evolving, and this is what creativity fosters. As we engage in creative processes, we learn to face uncertainty, embrace ambiguity, and adapt to changing circumstances. These are key traits of resilience.

The more you engage with creativity, the more you expand your ability to cope with whatever life throws your way. Whether you are writing a story to process your emotions or designing a new approach to your work challenges, creativity strengthens your ability to handle adversity. Through trial and error, creative exploration allows you to approach problems with curiosity rather than fear.

Ultimately, creativity transforms adversity into an opportunity for growth and learning. It encourages you to break free from old, limiting thought patterns and embrace new possibilities. It teaches you that you are not just a passive participant in life's struggles—you are an active creator, capable of shaping your world.

The act of creation—whether through art, problem-solving, or self-expression—is one of the most potent strategies for conquering life's modern challenges. By cultivating creativity, you not only find a way to manage stress and resolve conflicts, but you also build the resilience necessary to face future battles with confidence and innovation. In a world that is constantly evolving, creativity gives you the tools to not only adapt but to thrive. Embrace creativity as a weapon in your arsenal, and you will find that no challenge is too great to overcome.

The Warrior's Mindset

Throughout history, warriors have stood as the ultimate symbol of strength, discipline, and resilience. From the disciplined Stoic philosophers of Ancient Greece to the honorable Samurai of feudal Japan, warriors have long been revered for their ability to withstand adversity, face overwhelming odds, and emerge victorious. These warrior cultures didn't simply thrive on physical prowess or military tactics—they embodied mindsets that allowed them to endure hardship, adapt to challenges, and maintain their sense of purpose in the face of chaos. But how can we apply the ancient warrior mindset to the demands and struggles of modern life? This subchapter explores how to adapt the warrior ethos—particularly principles from Stoicism and Samurai ethics—to conquer modern-day challenges with honor, clarity, and resilience.

The warrior's mindset isn't about aggression or brute strength; it's about emotional control, strategic thinking, and an unwavering commitment to personal growth. In a world where stress, distractions, and uncertainties abound, the need for this mindset is greater than ever. In this subchapter, we'll examine the core philosophies of ancient warrior cultures, unpack their practical applications in today's world, and outline how you can use these teachings to conquer life's personal battles.

The Stoic Warrior: Embracing Control and Acceptance

One of the foundational elements of the warrior mindset comes from the philosophy of Stoicism, a school of thought popularized by ancient philosophers like Marcus Aurelius, Epictetus, and Seneca. Stoicism emphasizes the importance of focusing on what is within our control and accepting what lies outside of it. In the modern context, this philosophy is more relevant than ever as we navigate a world full of external pressures—everything from the demands of work to the constant bombardment of information.

The Stoic warrior is defined by emotional discipline. In the face of adversity, the Stoic doesn't lose control of their emotions. They do not let anger, frustration, or anxiety cloud their judgment. Instead, they cultivate an inner fortress of calm, remaining grounded in the present moment. When faced with a challenge, the Stoic asks themselves: *What is within my power to change? What can I control?* This simple yet powerful question enables them to direct their energy only toward that which they can influence, rather than being consumed by feelings of helplessness over things beyond their reach.

In the modern world, the Stoic mindset is a powerful antidote to stress and overwhelm. When faced with a difficult work project or personal dilemma, adopting the Stoic principle of control allows us to focus on taking practical, manageable steps rather than being paralyzed by anxiety. Whether it's a difficult boss, an impending deadline, or a personal setback, the Stoic warrior's first task is to assess the situation and focus on what they can do about it—without wasting energy on what they cannot control.

Exercise:

To begin integrating the Stoic mindset into your own life, consider keeping a daily journal. Each morning or evening, write down the challenges you are facing and categorize them into two columns: *What I can control* and *What I cannot control.* By doing this, you gain clarity and a sense of agency. You'll notice that the more you focus on the things within your power, the less power external forces have over your peace of mind.

The Samurai's Code: Honor, Discipline, and Self-Mastery

The Samurai, Japan's elite warrior class, followed a strict code of conduct known as *Bushido*, which emphasized honor, discipline, loyalty, and self-mastery. Although the Samurai were known for their fierce fighting skills, their true strength lay in their mental and emotional discipline. This code is particularly relevant in today's world, where personal integrity, consistency, and resilience are keys to long-term success.

One of the central tenets of Bushido is *seishin*, or the cultivation of a strong mind and spirit. The Samurai believed that the greatest battles were fought not on the battlefield, but within the self. To be a true warrior, they knew that mastery over their own impulses, desires, and emotions was essential. In a world filled with distractions—social media, temptations, and constant pressure—this aspect of the Samurai's ethos holds incredible value.

In modern life, *seishin* can be applied to our daily habits and routines. The constant noise and external stimuli we encounter every day make it easy to fall into a reactive mode, constantly chasing after the next distraction or fulfilling every desire. But the Samurai understood that true strength lay in mastering the mind, not allowing it to be swayed by every passing whim. By building mental resilience, we become less vulnerable to stress and more capable of taking purposeful action.

Another important aspect of *Bushido* is *rei*—respect. This principle was not just about respect for others, but respect for oneself. In a world where self-doubt and comparison often hinder progress, maintaining self-respect is vital. The Samurai didn't waste time on negativity or self-criticism. Instead, they cultivated a deep sense of respect for their own abilities and purpose, which fueled their drive to continuously improve.

Exercise:

To embody the spirit of Bushido in your daily life, start by cultivating a disciplined routine. Dedicate time each day to practice a skill or activity that enhances your mental clarity, such as meditation, physical exercise, or journaling. When you approach each task with the mindset of self-mastery, you begin to build the mental fortitude required to overcome modern-day challenges.

Courage in the Face of Fear: The Warrior's Greatest Weapon

Both the Stoic and the Samurai understood the importance of courage. However, courage in the context of the warrior's mindset is not the absence of fear; rather, it is the ability to act despite fear. This concept is critical in the modern world, where fear of failure, rejection, and the unknown often paralyze us from taking action.

The Stoic philosopher Seneca famously wrote, *"We suffer more in imagination than in reality."* This quote encapsulates the modern experience of fear. We fear what we don't know, and often our fear is based on imagined worst-case scenarios that never come to pass. The Stoic warrior faces these fears head-on by acknowledging them but refusing to be controlled by them. They take action in the face of fear, knowing that courage is not the absence of anxiety but the willingness to act in spite of it.

Similarly, the Samurai were trained to face death and danger with grace. The *bushido* code emphasized that a true warrior should fear nothing but dishonor. This doesn't mean they were invulnerable or immune to fear; rather, they had learned to transform fear into strength. They accepted that fear was a natural part of life, and rather than avoiding it, they chose to embrace it as a signal that they were on the right path.

Exercise:

To build courage in your own life, start by confronting one small fear each day. It could be something as simple as making a difficult phone call, saying "no" to an unreasonable request, or speaking up in a meeting. Gradually, as you face and conquer these smaller fears, you will build the courage needed to face larger challenges. Remember, the warrior's mindset is not about eliminating fear, but about learning to take action despite it.

Living with Purpose: The Warrior's Duty

At the heart of the warrior's mindset is a deep sense of purpose. The Stoics believed that living in accordance with nature and reason was the key to a meaningful life. For the Samurai, their service to their lord, their community, and their personal code of honor gave their lives a sense of direction and meaning. In modern life, the struggle to find purpose is one of the most significant battles many people face. With the overwhelming demands of work, relationships, and social obligations, it's easy to lose sight of what truly matters.

The warrior's purpose is not about external validation or material success. Instead, it is rooted in a personal mission—a commitment to self-improvement, service to others, and a quest for inner peace. The Stoic Marcus Aurelius wrote, *"The soul becomes dyed with the color of its thoughts."* If you allow your thoughts to be consumed with negativity, comparison, or failure, your life will reflect those qualities. But if you cultivate a mindset focused on purpose, growth, and service, your actions and your life will reflect those values.

Living with purpose is not about achieving an end goal; it's about engaging in meaningful work every day. Whether your purpose is to help others, improve yourself, or contribute to your community, the warrior's mindset requires that you live each day with intention and integrity.

Exercise:

To discover and connect with your own sense of purpose, take some time to reflect on your core values. What do you stand for? What principles guide your decisions? Write down your mission statement, and review it daily. As you go through your day, ask yourself if your actions align with that purpose. This ongoing reflection will help keep you on course, even when life presents its inevitable obstacles.

Becoming the Modern Warrior

The warrior's mindset is not reserved for ancient times or military leaders—it is a philosophy that can be applied to every aspect of modern life. By integrating Stoic principles, Samurai ethics, and the concept of courage, self-discipline, and purpose into your daily routine, you can conquer the challenges of modern life with grace, resilience, and strength.

The true power of the warrior lies not in fighting external battles but in mastering the internal ones—the struggles of fear, doubt, and uncertainty. By adopting the mindset of a warrior, you don't just face life's challenges; you transcend them, transforming every struggle into an opportunity for growth, purpose, and triumph.

Chapter 4: The Victory –
Living the Conquered Life

Embracing the 'Post-Victory Void'

Victory can be an overwhelming force. The moment you achieve what you've worked tirelessly toward—a promotion, a personal milestone, a long-held dream realized—it's easy to imagine that the sense of accomplishment will sustain you indefinitely. After all, this is what you've been striving for, right? Yet, paradoxically, many people find that even after the high of success, a sense of emptiness or confusion often follows. It's as if the finish line was never as fulfilling as the race itself. This feeling is real, and it's more common than you might think.

In this subchapter, we will explore why such a void appears after victory and how to embrace it rather than fear it. The key to true fulfillment after a personal conquest isn't simply in the victory itself but in how you navigate the space that follows. Conquering the post-victory void is about redefining what success really means, accepting the transient nature of achievement, and transforming that emptiness into an opportunity for new growth and purpose.

The Illusion of 'The Big Win'

We are conditioned by society to believe that success equals happiness. We are taught to think that achieving a major goal will finally provide us with the fulfillment, recognition, and internal peace we seek. Whether it's landing the perfect job, building a dream home, or completing a significant project, we expect the moment of success to be the pinnacle of our happiness. In reality, however, many people report feeling a sense of emotional whiplash when they finally achieve their goals. The very victory they have worked so hard for can trigger an unsettling feeling of uncertainty.

The truth is, victory is not a permanent solution to the inner emptiness that many of us feel. Success, in its traditional sense, offers a brief moment of celebration, followed by the inevitable question, "Now what?" This shift often leads to the "post-victory void"—a psychological space where the achievements you thought would bring satisfaction no longer seem enough.

It's essential to understand that success is not an eternal source of happiness. In fact, it is often a fleeting experience, and the rush of endorphins that come with it soon fades. If your happiness is anchored solely in external achievements, you'll find yourself in a constant cycle of chasing the next big thing without ever feeling truly content. The momentary satisfaction fades, and the hunger for something new takes over, leaving you with the void.

The Nature of the Void: Why It Exists

The "void" that follows success is not a void in the traditional sense. It's not the absence of everything, but rather the absence of *purpose* and *meaning*. When you pursue something for so long, there's a kind of singular focus—everything in your life revolves around that one goal, that one aspiration. Once you achieve it, you're left with the question: *What now?*

In the wake of victory, this lack of direction can feel like a vacuum. You've conquered your goal, but you haven't built a lasting foundation for a new sense of self. The void is a result of an overreliance on external achievements to define your sense of worth. When you achieve something monumental, it feels as though you've reached a peak, but the reality is that there are always new mountains to climb, new endeavors to pursue. The absence of that drive can feel hollow because we've spent so much of our time, energy, and identity wrapped up in the pursuit.

Another reason for this feeling is the misalignment between external success and internal peace. The world rewards us for external accomplishments—career advancements, financial prosperity, and social recognition—but rarely encourages us to cultivate internal peace and contentment. After a victory, you might be celebrated by those around you, but deep within, you may still feel unsettled, unsure, or even unfulfilled. The external validation doesn't always align with the internal growth required for long-term fulfillment.

Redefining Victory: From External to Internal Fulfillment

The key to conquering the post-victory void lies in rethinking what it means to be successful. If you define success as the constant accumulation of achievements, then you will inevitably feel a sense of emptiness when you stop and look around at what you've accomplished. But if you shift your definition of success from external markers to internal growth, then victory becomes a process rather than a destination. The question shifts from "What will make me happy?" to "How can I find deeper fulfillment in who I am becoming?"

Success, when viewed this way, is not about winning one single race but about engaging in an ongoing process of growth and evolution. It's about aligning your actions with your values and living in a way that reflects your authentic self, regardless of external approval or outcomes. In this framework, the void after victory becomes an invitation for deeper introspection, where you assess the long-term meaning behind what you've done and who you've become.

A key element of navigating this transition is self-reflection. When you achieve something monumental, take time to ask yourself what the victory means to you beyond the external validation. Did it bring you closer to your core values? Did it help you grow emotionally, intellectually, or spiritually? What lessons did you learn in the process of reaching that goal? These reflections help you transform the post-victory void into an opportunity for personal insight and continued development.

Exercise:

After a significant victory, take a moment to journal your thoughts. Ask yourself: *How has this achievement shaped who I am as a person? What have I learned through this journey that will help me in the future?* Rather than simply celebrating the accomplishment, dig deeper to explore the lessons it has taught you. Reflecting in this way helps you connect with your inner self, creating a sense of lasting fulfillment that isn't dependent on the external world.

Moving Beyond the Void: Finding Purpose in the Present

Once you've acknowledged the void and shifted your perspective on success, the next step is to establish a new purpose. It's essential not to allow yourself to stay stuck in the post-victory emptiness. This is where many people falter: they achieve their goal and then struggle to find meaning beyond it. Without a new direction, they feel lost.

One of the best ways to navigate this transition is to embrace the concept of continuous reinvention. Reinvention isn't about discarding the old version of yourself; it's about adding layers of growth, wisdom, and new experiences to your identity. When you've accomplished something significant, look at it as a stepping stone toward your next phase. Rather than focusing solely on external achievements, find ways to engage with new challenges and opportunities for growth. Take on new projects that excite you, engage in learning, and connect with people who inspire you.

This process of reinvention ensures that you don't fall into a rut or stop growing. It also helps you cultivate resilience because it teaches you that each success is a brief chapter in an ongoing story. There's always room for the next chapter, even after the most significant victory.

In fact, the post-victory void itself can be an incredible opportunity to discover new dimensions of yourself. It's in these moments of emptiness that you can ask deeper, more meaningful questions: *What do I truly value? What is my ultimate purpose?* These questions open the door to a more profound sense of fulfillment that goes beyond societal expectations or personal achievements. By embracing the void, you allow yourself to evolve into someone more resilient, adaptable, and fulfilled than before.

Exercise:

Set aside time every few months to assess your personal growth. Reflect on how you have changed since your last big victory. What have you learned? How have your values or goals shifted? This process of regular reflection helps you stay grounded in your own sense of purpose, ensuring that you do not fall into the trap of chasing external validation without understanding its deeper meaning.

Embracing the Cycle of Growth

Victory is a powerful force, but it is not the end of the journey. The post-victory void is not something to fear; it is a natural part of the process of growth. By redefining success, shifting your focus to internal fulfillment, and embracing the opportunity for continual reinvention, you can transcend the emptiness that sometimes follows victory. You can turn this moment into an opportunity for deeper introspection and new beginnings.

Remember that the true victory is not in reaching a single peak, but in how you navigate the entire journey of growth, learning, and self-discovery. The conquest of your challenges is only the beginning. How you embrace the victories, the voids, and the ongoing process of reinvention will define the true richness of your life. Through this cyclical process, you can conquer not just your goals but the very sense of purpose and fulfillment that will sustain you long after the applause fades.

The New Definition of Success

For many of us, success is a tangible target. We have been taught to view it as something external, something to be achieved, recognized, and validated. It's often measured in terms of wealth, status, career accomplishments, or societal acknowledgment. We envision success as a singular destination, a moment in time when everything aligns perfectly—when the promotion is earned, the house is bought, or the dream project is completed. And yet, once we attain these markers, we often find ourselves wondering, "Is this it? Is this really what I was striving for?"

This moment of realization—the questioning of what success truly means—often emerges in the aftermath of victory. It is a powerful moment, but it can also be unsettling. The external success you've achieved may not feel as fulfilling as you expected. There may be an unexpected emptiness, a nagging sense that something is missing. This is the moment when you must reconsider what success actually is, and perhaps redefine it for yourself in a way that brings deeper, more lasting fulfillment.

In this subchapter, we will delve into the process of creating a new definition of success—one that moves beyond the traditional metrics of achievement and incorporates a more holistic approach. We will explore how to shift from external validation to internal fulfillment, from societal benchmarks to personal values. This isn't just about rethinking success in theoretical terms; it's about changing the way you live your life, so that your victories are meaningful and your journey is fulfilling.

Moving Beyond External Success

The prevailing narrative in modern society is that success is something you achieve, something that can be earned, quantified, and displayed. External success is often defined by material gains: the size of your paycheck, the prestige of your job title, the brand of car you drive, or the number of followers you have on social media. These external markers are often held up as the gold standard of achievement, and we've internalized these standards as measures of our worth. In many cases, we chase after these accomplishments, believing that they will bring us happiness, fulfillment, and a sense of purpose.

However, this model of success has limitations. It fails to account for the intrinsic, internal aspects of our lives—the things that cannot be measured or bought. External success often does not satisfy our deeper needs for connection, meaning, and personal growth. When we define success solely in terms of what we acquire or accomplish, we risk missing the larger picture of who we are and who we want to become.

The gap between external success and internal fulfillment can be profound. We may achieve everything we thought we wanted, only to realize that it hasn't given us the peace, joy, or sense of purpose we were hoping for. This is why many people experience a form of emptiness after reaching their goals. The victory may feel hollow, because it was achieved according to someone else's definition of success.

True success, then, lies not in what you acquire, but in who you become in the process. It's about aligning your goals with your deeper values and pursuing a life that is authentic to your true self. When you measure success in terms of personal growth, well-being, and inner peace, you can begin to create a more sustainable, fulfilling version of success that lasts far beyond the accolades and possessions.

The Power of Personal Values

To shift your definition of success, you must start by clarifying your personal values. What truly matters to you? What do you want your life to stand for? These values form the foundation of your new definition of success. Unlike external achievements, which are often fleeting or dependent on circumstances, personal values are deep, enduring principles that can guide you throughout your life.

For example, you might value creativity, connection, growth, or service. If these are your core values, your definition of success will be rooted in how well you embody and express these values in your life. Success is no longer about earning a title or a paycheck—it's about living in alignment with your values, consistently choosing actions that reflect what truly matters to you.

This shift is powerful because it places the responsibility for success squarely within your own hands. It frees you from the cycle of chasing external rewards and instead anchors you in a sense of inner fulfillment. When you pursue success based on your values, each step you take, each action you perform, becomes an expression of who you are. This internal alignment allows you to feel a deep sense of satisfaction and meaning, regardless of external recognition.

Exercise:

Take a moment to write down your top five core values. Reflect on how these values show up in your life and how they can guide your definition of success moving forward. For each value, ask yourself: *How can I embody this value more fully in my daily life? What does success look like when I live according to this value?*

Embracing a Growth-Oriented Mindset

In addition to redefining success in terms of personal values, it is essential to shift your focus from fixed achievements to continuous growth. Traditional definitions of success often emphasize specific goals or outcomes—getting the promotion, finishing the novel, or acquiring a luxury item. These markers, while worthwhile, tend to reinforce the idea that success is a destination. Once you reach that destination, the journey is over, and the sense of fulfillment fades.

However, success is much more enriching when it is viewed as an ongoing process rather than a static endpoint. This mindset is rooted in the concept of growth, which is infinite and ever-evolving. No matter what you've achieved, there's always more room to grow, learn, and develop. Every victory is just one chapter in a never-ending story of personal transformation.

By embracing a growth-oriented mindset, you allow yourself to view success as a continuous journey, one that deepens over time. This shift opens up new possibilities for personal fulfillment. You no longer need to chase external recognition or measure your success solely by what you have accomplished. Instead, you measure your success by how much you have evolved, how much you continue to learn, and how much you contribute to others along the way.

This mindset helps you build resilience because it removes the pressure of reaching a final "finish line." Growth, by its nature, is a process—sometimes slow, sometimes nonlinear—but always moving forward. When you embrace this, each moment becomes an opportunity to improve, to push your limits, and to redefine what success means for you.

Shifting Focus from Acquisition to Contribution

Another key aspect of redefining success is shifting your focus from acquisition to contribution. In our society, we are often encouraged to think about success in terms of what we can gain—whether that's wealth, status, or possessions. But true fulfillment often comes from what we give to others and how we contribute to the world around us.

Success, in this sense, becomes less about personal gain and more about making a meaningful impact. This can take many forms: contributing to your community, creating something of value, mentoring others, or simply being present and compassionate in your relationships. When success is defined by contribution, it becomes a source of lasting satisfaction because it connects you to something greater than yourself.

Exercise:

Think about the ways in which you can contribute to others and to the world around you. What would it look like to prioritize giving over acquiring? How can you use your talents, skills, and resources to make a positive impact? Write down at least three ways you can increase your sense of contribution, both in your personal life and in your broader community.

Cultivating Peace and Purpose

At the heart of the new definition of success is the pursuit of peace and purpose. External success can bring fleeting moments of joy, but it rarely brings lasting peace. True fulfillment comes from living with intention, having a sense of purpose, and aligning your actions with your inner self. When you define success based on your own values, continuous growth, and meaningful contribution, you create a life that is purposeful and peaceful.

This peace doesn't come from achieving external milestones; it comes from knowing that you are living in accordance with what is most important to you. It comes from the knowledge that your actions reflect your values and contribute to the well-being of others. Peace arises when you stop chasing after validation and instead embrace the calm satisfaction of knowing that you are doing your best, growing steadily, and living authentically.

In this way, success becomes a state of being rather than a list of accomplishments. It's not about what you achieve, but about how you live—consciously, purposefully, and with peace. The new definition of success is about cultivating a life that feels fulfilling, meaningful, and in alignment with your deepest desires.

A Redefinition of Victory

As you redefine success, you free yourself from the need for external validation and embrace a deeper, more sustainable form of fulfillment. This new definition of success empowers you to live according to your values, pursue continuous growth, and contribute meaningfully to the world around you. It's not about what you acquire or achieve—it's about who you become and how you live. Success is no longer an endpoint, but a process, a state of being, and a journey that evolves as you do.

In redefining success, you have the power to create a life that truly reflects who you are and what you stand for. You can conquer the struggles of modern life by shifting your focus from external markers to internal fulfillment, from fleeting victories to long-term peace, purpose, and growth. This is the true victory—one that lasts, one that fulfills, and one that continues to evolve.

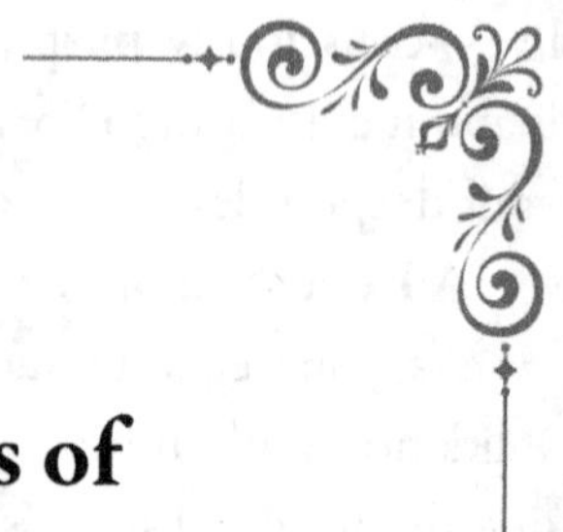

The Ongoing Process of Reinvention

The idea of reinvention is often misunderstood. In popular culture, it's often framed as a dramatic transformation—an overhaul of your entire identity, a total departure from the old and the introduction of the new. We think of famous stories of people who completely shift careers, change their lifestyles, or adopt entirely new identities in their quest for personal fulfillment. And while these stories can be inspiring, they also create a misconception about what real reinvention looks like.

The reality is, reinvention is not necessarily about radical, one-time shifts. In fact, the most successful reinvention is often incremental, a series of small, consistent changes over time. True reinvention is less about starting over from scratch and more about evolving, adapting, and continuously refining who you are in response to your life experiences and the world around you.

In this subchapter, we explore the ongoing process of reinvention. It's not about forcing a dramatic shift in your life but rather embracing change as a constant and necessary part of growth. As we navigate the complexities of modern life, we are faced with new challenges, new opportunities, and evolving circumstances that demand we adjust, adapt, and reinvent ourselves—not just once, but repeatedly, over the course of our lives. Reinvention, then, becomes a practice—a dynamic, lifelong process of becoming the best version of yourself.

The Evolution of Identity

When we think about reinvention, the idea of identity is central. Our sense of self is rarely fixed; it is a fluid, evolving construct shaped by our experiences, relationships, and internal growth. Over time, we adapt our sense of self based on the changes we go through. Whether it's a new job, the loss of a loved one, a shift in personal values, or an unexpected opportunity, our identity is constantly under construction. It evolves to meet the demands of the moment.

In the past, we might have relied on rigid social constructs or external milestones to define our identity. We defined ourselves by our jobs, our families, our social status, or even by the achievements we have accumulated. But in a rapidly changing world, those markers of identity are not always reliable. The things that once defined us—be it a professional title or a specific role in society—can suddenly shift, leaving us feeling disconnected or adrift.

Reinvention, then, involves embracing the fluidity of identity. Instead of clinging to an old sense of self, we must learn to embrace change and adjust our understanding of who we are. It's about becoming comfortable with the idea that your identity is not a static, unchanging thing. It's an ever-evolving concept that grows with you, adapting as you face new challenges, learn new things, and experience new phases in life. This fluid approach to identity allows you to be more adaptable, open to change, and ultimately more resilient in the face of life's inevitable twists and turns.

Exercise:

Take a moment to reflect on how your sense of self has evolved over the past few years. In what ways have you reinvented yourself? What roles or labels have you outgrown? Write down how your identity has shifted and what new aspects of yourself you want to explore moving forward.

The Role of Adaptability in Reinvention

Reinvention is closely linked to adaptability—the ability to adjust your mindset, behaviors, and even your values in response to changing circumstances. Adaptability is not just a survival mechanism; it's a tool for thriving in the face of adversity. As the world changes around us—whether due to shifts in the economy, technological advancements, or social movements—our capacity to adapt is what ultimately determines our success.

One of the challenges we face in modern life is the rapid pace of change. The world is evolving at a speed never before seen in human history, and this can create a sense of uncertainty or overwhelm. In such an environment, it's easy to feel like we're constantly trying to catch up, unable to fully grasp or control what's happening around us. But this uncertainty is not something to be feared. It's something to be embraced, for it offers us the opportunity to adapt, learn, and grow.

Adaptability is at the heart of reinvention. To reinvent yourself, you must be willing to change—to let go of old patterns of thinking, behaving, and perceiving. This requires an open mind and a willingness to let go of the need for control. It also means understanding that you are not defined by your past mistakes or failures. Reinvention is about viewing every challenge as an opportunity to grow, rather than as a sign of defeat.

This is particularly important in the context of modern life, where change is often inevitable and out of our control. We might lose a job, face unexpected health challenges, or experience disruptions in our personal lives. These events can feel like setbacks, but they are also moments where reinvention is possible. Instead of resisting change, we must learn to embrace it as a tool for growth.

Exercise:

Think about a recent change in your life that you initially resisted. How did you adapt to it, and what did you learn in the process? What lessons did this change teach you about yourself and your ability to reinvent? Write down the ways you can better embrace future changes, focusing on how adaptability can serve as a tool for growth.

Continuous Learning and Personal Growth

One of the most important aspects of reinvention is the commitment to continuous learning. The world around us is constantly evolving, and if we want to continue to evolve alongside it, we must adopt a mindset of lifelong learning. Reinvention is not a one-time event but an ongoing process of learning, unlearning, and relearning.

Personal growth doesn't happen by accident. It requires intentionality, curiosity, and a willingness to invest in your own development. To reinvent yourself, you must be proactive in seeking out opportunities for learning—whether through formal education, self-directed study, or simply by challenging your own assumptions and biases. Personal growth is a journey that requires constant reflection and evaluation. It's about looking at where you are and asking, "Where do I want to go next? What do I need to learn to get there?"

Continuous learning also means being open to feedback, both from others and from your own experiences. Reinvention requires a willingness to be vulnerable—to admit when you don't have all the answers and to seek guidance from those who have walked similar paths. It's about embracing mistakes as learning opportunities, rather than viewing them as failures. When you see mistakes as part of the process of reinvention, you can continue to move forward with confidence and clarity.

Exercise:

Commit to a new learning goal for the next six months. It could be a skill you want to acquire, a new area of knowledge you want to explore, or a personal habit you want to develop. Write down the steps you will take to achieve this goal and how it will contribute to your personal reinvention.

The Role of Purpose in Reinvention

At the heart of reinvention is the search for purpose. Reinvention is not just about changing who you are—it's about discovering who you are becoming and aligning your actions with your deeper sense of meaning and purpose. In many ways, reinvention is a quest for purpose—a way of redefining what matters most to you and how you want to contribute to the world.

In modern life, it's easy to get caught up in the hustle of everyday responsibilities and distractions. We may become so focused on survival—on getting through the day or meeting external expectations—that we lose sight of our deeper purpose. Reinvention, then, is a way of reconnecting with what truly matters to you, realigning your actions with your values, and refocusing on the things that give your life meaning.

Your purpose doesn't have to be something grandiose or world-changing. It could be something as simple as fostering deep, meaningful relationships, or using your skills to help others in your community. Reinvention is about aligning your life with your purpose, so that your actions feel meaningful and fulfilling. When you live in alignment with your purpose, reinvention becomes a natural process of growth and contribution.

Exercise:

Take a few moments to reflect on your current sense of purpose. How clear is it to you? Does your daily life reflect that purpose? If not, what small changes can you make to better align your actions with your deeper goals? Write down your reflections and any steps you can take to bring more purpose into your life.

The Fluidity of Reinvention

Reinvention is not a linear process, and it's important to recognize that it doesn't always unfold in predictable ways. Sometimes, it may involve setbacks or periods of confusion. These moments of uncertainty are not failures—they are simply part of the process. The key is to remain open to change and growth, and to understand that reinvention is an ongoing, cyclical process.

Just as the seasons change and the world around us shifts, so too does our own evolution. Reinvention allows us to keep moving forward, even when we don't have all the answers. It's about trusting that, with time, reflection, and adaptability, we can continue to grow and evolve in meaningful ways.

Reinvention is not a destination; it's a continuous journey. It is the practice of embracing change, learning constantly, and aligning your life with your purpose. The ongoing process of reinvention ensures that you remain resilient, adaptable, and engaged in the process of personal growth. In a world that is constantly shifting, reinvention allows you to navigate life's challenges and triumphs with grace, strength, and purpose.

The Victory of Peace

We often think of victory as the end point—the culmination of a long journey of struggle and effort. When we conquer a major challenge or achieve a significant goal, it's natural to assume that we have reached the destination. Our society, which celebrates external success through awards, recognition, and social status, often reinforces this idea that victory equals completion. However, this understanding of victory can be deceptive.

In reality, the true victory is not about simply achieving a goal or reaching the peak of success—it's about finding peace within ourselves. It's about navigating life's complexities with grace and confidence, embracing the internal calm that allows us to thrive beyond the struggle. The paradox of modern life is that, despite all our efforts, triumph without inner peace often leads to emptiness or dissatisfaction. This subchapter explores how the greatest victory of all is the one where you find peace—peace within yourself, peace in your relationships, and peace in your purpose.

The Illusion of External Success

In our modern world, success is often defined by external markers: wealth, social status, recognition, or material possessions. These goals, while important in certain contexts, can become a trap. When we define our self-worth by what we achieve externally, we set ourselves up for perpetual dissatisfaction. The pursuit of external success can be a relentless chase that never truly ends, leaving us feeling perpetually incomplete.

The reality is that external markers of success can provide fleeting moments of fulfillment, but they do not guarantee lasting peace. Even when we achieve what we thought would bring us happiness—whether it's a promotion, a new house, or recognition in our field—we often find ourselves asking, "Is this it? What now?" This is the paradox: the pursuit of external success may deliver short-term rewards, but it rarely offers long-term peace.

True victory lies not in the accumulation of accolades but in the internal satisfaction of knowing that we are aligned with our values, living with purpose, and at peace with who we are. The desire for external recognition may be part of human nature, but we must learn to balance this desire with a deeper understanding of what truly brings us fulfillment—inner peace.

Finding Inner Peace in the Midst of Struggle

Inner peace is not a state of perfection. It doesn't mean the absence of challenges or discomfort; rather, it is the ability to navigate life's inevitable ups and downs with resilience and calmness. Peace is found not by avoiding struggle but by cultivating the capacity to endure it without being consumed by it. It's the ability to remain grounded and centered, regardless of the external circumstances.

In the modern world, peace can seem elusive. We are constantly bombarded by information, distractions, expectations, and pressures. There is always something to be done, something to be improved, someone to impress. The pressure to keep moving forward, to continue succeeding, can be overwhelming. In such an environment, peace may seem like an impossible ideal—something we can never fully attain.

However, peace is not a destination but a practice. It is not about creating a life without challenges or struggles but learning to coexist with them in a way that doesn't disturb your internal equilibrium. The key to finding peace is learning how to respond to life with equanimity—developing the ability to face difficulties with calm and poise.

This doesn't mean ignoring the difficulties or pretending they don't exist. On the contrary, inner peace requires us to confront the struggles of life head-on, to acknowledge them and to deal with them with a sense of mindfulness and acceptance. It's about cultivating an attitude of acceptance and understanding, where we don't resist life's natural ebb and flow, but flow with it.

The Power of Acceptance and Surrender

A significant part of achieving inner peace is learning to let go. This concept, often counterintuitive in a world that values control, is essential for conquering modern life's struggles. We often think that to succeed, we must always be in control of our circumstances, our emotions, and the outcomes of our actions. We grasp at outcomes and resist uncertainty, thinking that only by controlling every aspect of our lives can we find peace.

However, this drive for control often leads to anxiety, frustration, and burnout. The truth is, there are many aspects of life that are beyond our control—other people's actions, unexpected events, or the outcomes of our efforts. Trying to control these elements only adds stress to our lives, preventing us from experiencing true peace.

To find peace, we must learn to surrender—not in the sense of giving up or avoiding responsibility, but in the sense of releasing the need to control everything. Surrendering means accepting that there will always be uncertainty, that not everything will go according to plan, and that life's outcomes are not always in our hands. When we let go of the need to control, we free ourselves from the anxiety that comes with it, and we open ourselves up to the peace that comes from simply being in the moment.

This act of surrender is not a weakness but a strength. It is an acknowledgment that we are part of something larger than ourselves—that we do not need to control everything in order to thrive. Instead, we must trust the process of life, knowing that peace comes from embracing the unknown and finding calm in the midst of it.

Exercise: Letting Go of Control

Identify an area of your life where you feel the need to control outcomes. Reflect on how this need for control is affecting your peace of mind. How can you begin to release this control and allow life to unfold naturally? Write down the steps you can take to surrender the need for perfection and trust that things will work out, even if they don't go exactly as planned.

Peace in Relationships

Another key aspect of the victory of peace is the peace we cultivate in our relationships. In today's interconnected world, relationships are often strained by external pressures—work demands, social media expectations, or a lack of time and attention. We often find ourselves caught in cycles of conflict, misunderstanding, or emotional withdrawal, which erode our sense of peace.

Peace in relationships doesn't mean the absence of conflict. Conflict is a natural part of any relationship, and learning to navigate it with respect and understanding is part of the journey toward inner peace. Instead, peace in relationships means cultivating empathy, setting healthy boundaries, and practicing active listening. It means choosing to respond with kindness, even in moments of frustration or disagreement, and learning to let go of the need to be "right."

It also means letting go of expectations. In many relationships, we have a tendency to project our own desires and needs onto others, expecting them to fulfill our emotional needs or to behave in ways that meet our expectations. When those expectations are not met, it leads to disappointment and tension. Learning to let go of these expectations—while still maintaining healthy standards—can significantly reduce conflict and increase the peace we experience in our relationships.

Peace in relationships also involves forgiveness—not just of others, but also of ourselves. Holding onto grudges, past hurts, or mistakes prevents us from experiencing peace. Forgiveness is not about excusing wrong behavior; it's about releasing ourselves from the burden of resentment and allowing healing to occur.

Exercise: Cultivating Peace in Relationships

Think about a relationship in your life where there is tension or conflict. What expectations do you have of this person that might be contributing to the tension? How can you release these expectations and approach the relationship with more empathy and understanding? Write down your thoughts and create an action plan for improving the peace in this relationship.

The Peace of Purpose

True peace is found in alignment with a deeper sense of purpose. When we live in accordance with our values, passions, and purpose, we experience a profound sense of peace. This sense of peace comes not from avoiding difficulty but from knowing that we are living authentically and contributing to something larger than ourselves.

In the pursuit of success, we often get caught up in external achievements, thinking that our worth is defined by what we accomplish. However, the greatest source of peace comes from knowing that we are living in alignment with our deeper values and purpose. When we are true to ourselves and our mission in life, we feel more at peace, regardless of the external circumstances.

Purpose gives us direction, meaning, and fulfillment. It's what helps us navigate life's challenges with resilience and strength. Even in difficult times, a clear sense of purpose can provide a sense of peace, as it reminds us that we are part of a larger journey, one that is meaningful and worth pursuing.

Exercise: Defining Your Purpose

Take some time to reflect on your purpose in life. What are the core values and passions that guide you? How can you align your daily actions with this purpose? Write down your purpose statement and commit to taking small steps each day to live in accordance with it.

The True Triumph is Peace

The victory of peace is not about the absence of struggle but the ability to find calm and clarity in the midst of life's inevitable challenges. It's about learning to navigate the chaos of the modern world with grace and resilience, trusting in the process of life, and cultivating a sense of purpose and connection that anchors you in times of uncertainty.

In the end, the true triumph is not external success but inner peace. It is the peace that comes from knowing that, no matter what happens, you are grounded in your values, at peace with yourself, and living with purpose. It is this peace that allows you to thrive beyond the struggle, to rise above the chaos, and to truly conquer the challenges of modern life.

Conclusion: The Eternal Cycle of Conquest

We are born into a world that seems to be in perpetual motion, where success is often marked by a series of struggles, wins, losses, and reinventions. Yet, in the modern landscape, with its barrage of demands, distractions, and internal battles, the true question is not whether we will face struggles, but how we will face them. The essence of this journey—the very heart of "Veni, Vidi, Vici"—lies in understanding that conquest is not a singular event, but a continuous process. Victory, as we have seen, is not the end. It is a new beginning, a step into an ongoing cycle of growth and renewal. Like the great conquerors of history, our path is never one of finality. It is a life lived in cycles of learning, confronting new challenges, redefining success, and, above all, cultivating resilience.

The Endless Battle: Embracing the Process

As we stand at the conclusion of this journey, one thing becomes clear: the struggle never truly ends. Life's battles are cyclical. Just as Julius Caesar's triumphs were punctuated by wars, challenges, and defeats, our victories too are part of an endless cycle. To frame this idea differently, we might look at it as the seasons of life: each victory, no matter how significant, marks the end of one phase and the beginning of the next. After each victory, there is always the inevitable emptiness—the sense of "What now?" The great conquerors of the past understood that their achievements were not endpoints but transitions. And so must we.

The real key to conquering modern life lies not in expecting a final, all-encompassing victory but in learning to embrace the process itself. Each victory brings us one step closer to the next phase, which will inevitably come with new challenges. Understanding this truth releases us from the myth of the "final win." Instead of seeking to be free from challenges forever, we learn to navigate them more effectively. We embrace the constant ebb and flow of victories and setbacks. Through this, we develop an understanding that life's struggles are not interruptions to our happiness but opportunities for further growth.

We cannot afford to view our challenges as anomalies to be defeated and moved beyond. In fact, the challenges we face in life are a defining part of the human experience. They shape us, challenge us, and build the foundation of our future success. This is where resilience becomes key: embracing each battle, small or large, as an opportunity to grow stronger.

The Warrior's Legacy: Conquering for a Higher Purpose

As we engage with life's battles, we must ask ourselves a fundamental question: Why are we fighting? Conquering, whether it's a personal struggle or a societal challenge, is rarely an isolated endeavor. It is rarely for personal glory or wealth. Instead, it's about creating a legacy—a story bigger than ourselves. The mindset of "Veni, Vidi, Vici" isn't just about personal triumph; it's about becoming a force for change. It's about extending the power of our victories to others and contributing to the world around us in meaningful ways.

This is where the concept of "living the conqueror's legacy" becomes truly transformative. The victories we achieve aren't just for our own benefit. When we conquer personal struggles, we gain the tools, mindset, and resilience to help others. Conquering becomes an act of service—an opportunity to model the power of growth, change, and resilience. Just as warriors of old passed their knowledge and strategies down through generations, we too can leave a legacy of strength, courage, and a deep understanding of human struggle.

This legacy can manifest in many forms—through our work, our relationships, and our communities. The triumphs of today can shape the future of others if we choose to pass on the knowledge, resilience, and mindset that helped us overcome our struggles. If you wish to truly conquer, then conquer for others. Use your struggles to light the way for those who follow, and pass along the tools and wisdom that allowed you to overcome the challenges you faced.

The warrior's legacy isn't about imposing power. It's about leaving a lasting imprint of hope, strength, and endurance. It's about showing others that victory isn't about avoiding hardship, but about learning how to face it with grace and fortitude.

Building a Legacy of Resilience, Growth, and Purpose

The cyclical nature of conquest, and the understanding that each victory is part of a larger journey, invites us to continuously grow, evolve, and redefine what success means. And as we build upon each victory, we shift from seeing ourselves as mere survivors of modern life to becoming true creators of our destiny.

Resilience, growth, and purpose are the building blocks of this legacy. The legacy we leave is not written in grand achievements but in the day-to-day moments when we choose to persevere despite setbacks, when we rise again after falling, and when we choose to serve others with the knowledge and strength we have gained through our struggles.

By embracing the process of constant renewal, we learn to live with purpose, knowing that every moment is an opportunity to advance. Just as the warrior always prepares for the next battle, so too must we always be preparing for the next phase of growth. Purpose gives us direction—it's the compass that guides us through the endless cycle of victory and struggle. When we align our actions with our deepest values, we can conquer even the toughest of battles with resilience and focus.

The Mindset of the Modern Warrior

Throughout everything, we must return to the idea of the modern warrior. The warrior mindset embraces adversity as an opportunity to develop stronger. It is about accepting that life's conflicts, whether internal or external, are unavoidable. It is about realizing that we will always confront obstacles and struggles—and that these are not to be dreaded, but rather welcomed. Warriors do not shy away from conflict. They confront it full on, demonstrating discipline, guts, and wisdom.

This worldview does not necessitate anger or violence, as ancient warriors previously shown. Instead, it invites us to confront the challenges of modern life with mental, emotional, and physical fortitude. The fighter is capable of overcoming distractions, learning from mistakes, and continuing to grow in the face of adversity. They live with intention, understanding that every action, decision, and moment is important.

We must embrace this perspective if we want to be victors in our own right. Our wars are fought not with swords, but with decisions, habits, and perseverance. We are battling for more than simply personal success—a legacy of strength, progress, and purpose that will inspire others.

The Triumph of Peace

Finally, in our constant quest to master life's challenges, we must never forget the ultimate win—the victory of peace. Conquering modern-day issues entails more than merely gaining outward success or overcoming personal challenges. It is, above all, about achieving inner serenity. The ultimate conqueror is the person who finds peace within themselves, despite the chaos around them. The paradox of triumph is that once we have won the exterior wars, we must turn inward to conquer ourselves. True serenity is the cornerstone for long-term prosperity. It is the realization that we are enough exactly as we are. It is the peaceful assurance that comes from knowing we are resilient, capable of adapting to any situation, and that our worth is not determined by our triumphs or failures. Peace occurs when we no longer require external affirmation, when we are confident in our own skin, and when we understand that life's challenges are not obstacles, but stepping stones. The ultimate lesson of "Veni, Vidi, Vici" is that victory is more than just one event. It's a process—an ongoing cycle of triumph, growth, and evolution. And the final triumph is not in what we accomplish, but in how we live our lives afterward. It is in our power to move forward, to create something bigger than ourselves, and to live in accordance with our highest purpose. This is the genuine legacy of modern conquerors. As you finish this book and reflect on your journey, remember that you are both a warrior and a conqueror, navigating an infinite cycle of growth, obstacles, and achievements. Accept the challenge and live your life with a purpose. Always find serenity inside oneself. This is a true victory. This is how you overcome the challenges of modern life.

Don't miss out!

Visit the website below and you can sign up to receive emails whenever JULIAN KANE publishes a new book. There's no charge and no obligation.

https://books2read.com/r/B-A-ABSYC-JSBKF

BOOKS2READ

Connecting independent readers to independent writers.